LIVING WITH THE LAND

DESERT, RAIN-FOREST, ARCTIC, AND PLAINS REGIONS

MARY SHANLEY GATES & LUCY DE MARIA LA POINTE

Good Year Books

An Imprint of Addison-Wesley Educational Publishers, Inc.

Good Year Books are available for most basic curriculum subjects plus many enrichment areas. For more Good Year Books, contact your local bookseller or educational dealer. For a complete catalog with information about other Good Year Books, please write:

Good Year Books
1900 East Lake Avenue
Glenview, IL 60025

Design by Nancy Rudd.

ISBN 0-673-36397-X
1 2 3 4 5 6 7 8 9 - BW - 04 03 02 01 00 99 98 97 96

DEAR COLLEAGUE:

There is an old Chinese proverb that says, "If you give a man a fish, you feed him for a day. If you teach a man to fish, you feed him for a lifetime." We believe that education is a lifelong process of investigation and learning. That is why the lessons in this book are constructed to actively engage students in their own learning. We can give students information, but it is more rewarding when they discover the information for themselves. The challenges set forth in each lesson will stimulate their curiosity while reinforcing learning skills.

Living with the Land covers four regions of the Earth's surface: desert, rain forest, arctic, and plains. (The section on plains deals with the Great Plains of the United States due to the relevance of U.S. history to the social studies curriculum taught at the intermediate level.) Students will investigate diverse cultures, geography, and ecosystems. Principles based on national curriculum standards from various subject areas have been incorporated into the lessons. We emphasize nonfiction reading skills, such as research and note-taking, since today's students are required to consult and derive meaning from more sources than any group of learners in the past. We urge you to utilize all available

---

Making Text Meaningful

Nonfiction Reading → **Note-Taking** → **Nonfiction Writing**

- Sort.
- Stay on topic.
- Categorize.
- Identify key words and phrases.
- Reorganize.
- Put information in your own words to cement meaning.

technologies, from books to the Internet. All traditional subject areas are represented in each section, but learning skills are integrated, much as they are in our daily lives.

The book contains ten lessons on each region. The format is easy to follow, whether you are a first-year teacher or a veteran of thirty years. Each lesson includes objectives and step-by-step directions. Some lessons may be conducted in a class period, but others will require more time for investigation. Each lesson ends with ideas to extend activities. Lesson design varies, including individual, partner, and cooperative group instruction. A region summary is listed at the beginning of each unit, while you'll find a student glossary at the end of each unit. You may wish to provide copies for students as you begin unit instruction. Make modifications based on your classroom needs. Resources for each unit are listed in the bibliography.

May you and your students enjoy the pleasurable pursuit of knowledge!

Respectfully yours,

Mary Shanley Gates and Lucy De Maria La Pointe

LESSON	CONTENT AREA	SKILLS

DESERT REGIONS

LESSON	CONTENT AREA	SKILLS
Desert Similes	language arts	using reference materials
Desert Winds	geography	map skills
Desert Faces	reading/writing connection	note taking
Ship of the Desert	reading	locate/summarize information
Experiments with Variables	science	predict outcome/record results
Pharaoh's Lost Tomb	geography	using compass rose; cardinal directions
San or Tourist Point of View	language arts	supporting opinion
The Mighty Saguaro	listening	note-taking skills/point of view
The Flying Stick	math	gathering/graphing data
Water of Life	reading	research/project skills

RAIN-FOREST REGIONS

LESSON	CONTENT AREA	SKILLS
Rain-Forest Mobile Research	reading	research/note taking
The Great Kapok Tree	science/reading	contrasting environments
Advance Warning	science/reading	vocabulary/using limited prior knowledge
Global Alert!	reading/writing connection	newspaper writing
You Are What You Eat	science	nutrition comparison
Atlas Fact-Finding Mission	reading/geography	graphic organizer
South American Cities	geography	scale/estimating distance
Rain-Forest Fractions	math	interpreting information
Turn It Around	language arts	word analysis/antonyms
People of the Rain Forest	anthropology	problem-solving strategies

LESSON	CONTENT AREA	SKILLS
ARCTIC REGIONS		
A Picture Is Worth a Thousand Words	reading	prereading
Igloo Blueprint	math	measurement, fraction, and geometry
Arctic Alliteration	language arts	parts of speech
Perishable Peas	science	experiment using scientific method
Ancient Artifacts	archaeology	research skills
Making Tracks	science	research skills
All Dressed Up	reading/writing connection	research skills
Arctic Circle	geography	map skills
Polar Glow	science	compare and contrast
Whale Watchers	science/geography	map skills
PLAINS REGIONS		
The Disappearing Buffalo	reading/math	graphing data
Legends of Long Ago	reading/writing connection	story writing
Scaled Down to Size	geography	scale of measurement
Journal Journeys	reading/writing connection	research/note taking
Changing Times	history	research skills
The Shrinking Land	thinking/application skills	using criteria
To Your Health	science	research skills
Bountiful Bison	reading	organization skills
Animal Adventures	math/research	creating word problems
True Treaty	thinking skills	conflict resolution

CONTENTS

ARCTIC REGIONS

PLAINS REGIONS

DESERT
REGIONS

Desert regions are found on all continents except Europe. Deserts receive little precipitation, usually less than ten inches a year. Some regions become deserts because mountains block precipitation or because they are too far from the ocean for rain-laden clouds to reach them. Deserts can be hot, like the Kalahari in Africa, or cold, like the Gobi in Asia. Antarctica is the largest cold desert region in the world.

Desert temperatures vary greatly. In the Sahara desert, temperatures range from a scorching 120 degrees in the day to freezing at night. Plants and animals in desert regions have developed adaptations to conserve water. Most predators hunt at night, when temperatures are cooler. The kangaroo rat may live its entire life without drinking water, obtaining needed moisture from the grain it eats. The ribs of a saguaro cactus swell to store water during dry periods. The oasis, a fertile area around a well or an underground spring, has always been a refuge for desert-dwelling animals.

People who are native to desert regions are nomadic. They travel in search of food for themselves and their livestock. The Bushmen, or San, of the Kalahari are hunters and gatherers. The Bedouin of the Sahara are herders who raise goats and camels.

Modern technology has helped people to cultivate desert regions. Dams such as the Aswan in Egypt or pipeline systems like those found in California aid crop production. Mideastern countries have built desalination plants to turn salt water into fresh water. Plastic greenhouses and advanced watering systems allow countries like Israel to produce most of their own food. However, desertification, or the expansion of deserts, is a problem today. The effect of desertification on global weather patterns concerns modern scientists.

DESERT REGIONS

DESERT SIMILES

OBJECTIVE

The purpose of this lesson is to assess student knowledge about the desert environment and to use reference materials to help stimulate interest at the beginning of the unit.

PROCEDURE

1. Tell students to close their eyes for 30 seconds and to envision a desert scene. Encourage them to use all their senses.

2. Ask students to think of adjectives to describe the desert. List the words on the chalkboard or use an overhead projector.

3. Review with students the structure of a simile: a comparison using the words *like* or *as*.

4. Have students complete the Desert Similes worksheet individually, in pairs, or in groups. Students will need a thesaurus or dictionary to complete the worksheet. Provide time for images to be shared.

EXTENSIONS

1. Toward the end of the unit, have students create similes for specific tribes, plants, and animals of the desert. Example: *The aborigine's spear was as sharp as . . . .*

2. Have students use a thesaurus to find synonyms or antonyms for some of the words on the class list.

3. Use the class similes and illustrations to create a coloring book to share with a younger class.

4. Review the format of a metaphor and have the class convert selected similes into metaphors.

5. Brainstorm a list of special effects to go with the similes, such as steam or crackling paper for heat. Have the students read their similes with special effects, and capture the readings on a tape recorder.

DESERT SIMILES

Name(s) _____

A simile is a comparison using the words *like* or *as*.

Complete the similes below.

The desert is as *dry* as _____.

Like _____ , the sun beat down on the caravan.

At night, the chilling cold of the desert feels like _____.

The sand *stretched* before me like _____.

The spines on the cactus were as *sharp* as _____.

Like a _____ , the sidewinder slithered away.

Use a thesaurus or dictionary to replace the italicized words.

Create a desert simile of your own, and illustrate it in the space below.

_____

DESERT WINDS

OBJECTIVE

The purpose of this lesson is for students to practice map skills by locating information about deserts in varied resources, particularly atlases.

PROCEDURE

1. Choose a variety of deserts from around the globe. Some possible choices are the Sahara, Namib, Atacama, Great Sandy, Sonoran, Kalahari, and Gobi.

2. Divide the class into learning groups. Assign roles or have students choose them. Possible roles are reader, information-finder, agreement-checker, and writer.

3. Give the group the name of a desert to research, and tell them to keep it secret from other groups. Using a variety of sources, particularly maps, the group should locate "clues" and write them in the spaces provided on the Desert Winds sheet.

4. When everyone is done, the groups exchange sheets. Students should try to find the name of the desert using the clues provided.

5. Have the class discuss whether any symbols on the maps helped them locate deserts, what sources were easiest to use, and what sources were most helpful.

EXTENSIONS

1. Modify the lesson to describe other geographical features, such as mountains, rivers, or rain forests.

2. Choose one desert for the class to research. Assign each group a research topic, such as climate, mammals, insects, birds, reptiles, tribes, or plants. Have students find three to five fascinating facts about the topic. Students should copy the facts onto 3-by-11-inch strips of colored paper. Use the strips to create a bulletin board titled "BELIEVE IT OR NOT!" Enhance the board with student illustrations.

DESERT WINDS

Clue Givers: _____   Clue Finders _____

A sirocco, or desert wind, has blown the clues to the name of this desert all over the page. Using the clues provided, an atlas, and other sources, fill in the name of the desert below.

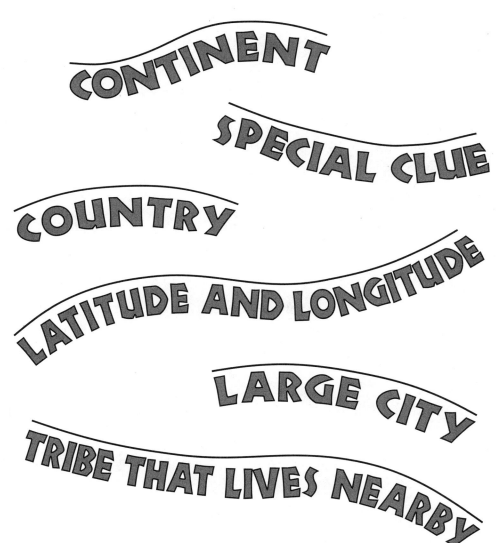

CONTINENT

SPECIAL CLUE

COUNTRY

LATITUDE AND LONGITUDE

LARGE CITY

TRIBE THAT LIVES NEARBY

Desert name: _____

DESERT FACES

OBJECTIVE

This lesson will reinforce note-taking skills while introducing students to three tribes that live in separate desert regions.

PROCEDURE

1. Ask students if they know of a group of people whose daily life depends on what is found in the environment. Any group that has already been discussed in class is appropriate.

2. Tell students that they are going to learn about three tribes that live in desert regions.

3. Compare the lives of students with the lives of a nomadic desert tribe. How are they similar or different?

4. Read together or independently the Desert Faces sheet.

5. Discuss note-taking skills, and remind students to locate key words and phrases and to stay on the topic.

6. Have students fill in the chart comparing the lives of three tribes.

7. After students have finished, either on an overhead or the chalkboard, fill in a class chart together. Review key words, phrases, and facts found.

EXTENSIONS

1. Assign students a particular tribe to research, and create a visual project display.

2. Compare student life with desert tribal life, using the same or a different chart.

3. Create a bulletin board with pictures of desert environments and people adapting to them.

4. Have students write an acrostic poem about a desert region.

5. Extend research into different categories, such as artifacts, transportation, and religion.

DESERT FACES

Name(s) _____

Many different tribes live in the deserts.

Some are the

Tuareg	**Mongol**
San (Bushman)	**Bedouin**
Navaho	**Hopi**
Aborigine	**Papago**

Pick three tribes, and fill in the chart with notes about their daily lives.

Use any sources available. Just write key words and phrases.

TRIBE	ENVIRONMENT	SHELTER	FOOD

SHIP OF THE DESERT

OBJECTIVE

The purpose of this lesson is to have students find and summarize pertinent information about camels in the Sahara.

PROCEDURE

1. Divide the class into learning groups. Assign roles or have students choose them. Possible roles are reader, highlighter, agreement-checker, writer, and sharer.

2. Provide each group with a copy of the text and graphics pages for Ship of the Desert.

3. Have students read the text out loud, without stopping.

4. Then have students reread the text silently, highlighting specific information about the camel that belongs in the caption boxes. Have students rewrite the information in their own words.

5. When everyone is done, provide time for group sharing. Note how information may be worded differently but still contain common facts.

EXTENSIONS

1. Have students do additional research on dromedaries and other camels, making a chart showing their similarities and differences.

2. Have students write a story about a young Bedouin boy who is learning to raise camels.

3. Enlarge the camel on page 12, and prepare a class bulletin board.

4. Consult your county agricultural department or local museum to see if there is a wool weaver in your area. Invite the weaver to demonstrate the craft to your class, or arrange a field trip.

5. Brainstorm a list of the varied uses of wool in our daily lives.

SHIP OF THE DESERT

Name(s) _____

Yuu're in the Sahara Desert surrounded by sand dunes. The scorching sun is beating down on you. The nearest village is ten kilometers away. There's not an oasis in sight, and your canteen is almost empty. Do you panic? No way! You're riding a camel, one of the most reliable forms of transportation in the desert.

The camel is often called "the ship of the desert." While it doesn't look like a ship, the camel has been carrying people and goods across seas of sand for centuries. Camels may look awkward with their skinny legs and long, curved necks, but nature has provided them with special features that protect them in the harsh desert environment.

The dromedary, or one-hump camel, has been used for transportation in northern Africa for thousands of years. The hump is made of stored fat, which the camel can use on long journeys where food is scarce. Camels have tough skin in their mouths, so they can eat prickly desert plants too. Their flat feet help them walk safely on shifting sand. The long, skinny legs raise the main part of the camel's body above the sand to where the air is a bit cooler.

Camels can carry hundreds of pounds on their backs. Steadily, they plod along, over scorching sand and in temperatures well above 100 degrees. Years ago, groups of camels carrying goods—called caravans—would travel a hundred miles each day. The caravan leaders tried to camp at night near an oasis or community well. Here the travelers watered and fed the animals. A thirsty camel could drain a twenty-gallon fish tank in about ten minutes. Most people drink less than one gallon of water during an entire day!

Deserts seldom get rain, but violent sandstorms can block out the sun. The camel has hair inside its ears, bushy eyebrows, and

a double row of eyelashes to keep out sand. Camels can even tighten the muscles in their noses to prevent swirling sand from getting inside.

The two-humped or Bactrian camel lives in the Gobi Desert of Asia. Bactrian camels also store fat in their humps. This is helpful because the winters are cold, and food is not always available. Two-humped camels grow thick fur in winter to protect them from bitter temperatures. Like other mammals, they shed this coat in spring when the weather gets warmer.

Tribes like the Bedouin of the Sahara need the camel to survive, much like the Native American tribes of the Plains that depended on the buffalo. Camel hair is woven into cloth. The cloth is used to make tents and rugs that protect people from sun, wind, and sand. Camels provide milk with high vitamin C content. Occasionally, camels are used for meat. Dried camel droppings are burned as fuel in cooking fires and for heat, just as buffalo dung was used by Native American tribes.

Today there are easier ways to transport goods and people across the desert. Jets, trucks, and trains are much faster than camels. But to the people who still live in the desert as their ancestors did long ago, the camel is important. To them, this "ship of the desert" will never go out of style.

SHIP OF THE DESERT

Name _____

Read the article. Highlight information you think should go in the boxes. Summarize this information in your own words. Write you notes in the correct boxes.

EXPERIMENT WITH VARIABLES

OBJECTIVE

The purpose of this lesson is for students to understand the concept of variables, to conduct an experiment using variables, and to predict outcomes based on polar coordinates.

PROCEDURE

1. Gather experiment materials for each group of students:

    • 8- or 9-inch aluminum pie plates or aluminum salad-bar containers with higher sides than a plate

    • Straws (one per group member)

    • A half cup of fine sand (can be bought at a craft store; buy colored sand for the projects listed in the extensions)

    • Newspaper to cover the work area

    NOTE: All students should have the same size straws and plates for consistency.

2. Divide the class into groups. Review the ways sand is moved, that is, by wind and rain. Explain the difference between constants, things that don't change, and variables, things that do change. An example is the classroom environment: the room itself does not change, but the people in it and the arrangement of furniture do.

3. On the chalkboard, review the use of degrees when giving directions. Then have each group label their plate with masking tape:

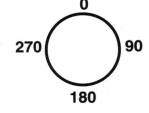

4. Tell the students that they will experiment with constants and variables to see how each could affect the desert environment. Spread newspaper on the desk, and pass out the experiment materials. Shake the plates to level the sand.

5. Tell students that one person in the group is going to rest the top of the straw on the edge of the plate and blow for three seconds. What do they think will happen? Instruct each group to fill out the prediction on the record sheet for the first experiment.

From *Living with the Land*, Copyright © 1998 Good Year Books.

On your count, have students blow into the straw for three seconds. Provide time for students to record results in the results section for the first experiment.

Ask students to name the constants in this experiment, which are the amount of sand, distance, and time. Have them name the variables in this experiment, which are the direction and force of breath. Encourage the groups to discuss possible variables and the effects of each before having them complete the second experiment independently. Remind them to complete the first section prior to conducting the actual experiment and recording the results.

6. Share and compare results. Lead students in a discussion of how variables might affect a desert environment.

EXTENSIONS

1. Study the designs and the purposes of sand painting by Native American tribes from the Southwest, and then have students create original designs on paper plates. Display the finished art on bulletin boards.

2. Have students make abstract designs with glue on oaktag and then blow sand across the design using a straw.

3. Study the Badlands of South Dakota. Create a game in which the players must use polar coordinates to navigate their way through a maze on the game board.

4. Ask students to collect, compare, and display maps that use polar and rectangular grid formats.

5. Discuss the effects of important variables in other environments, such as rainfall in tropical regions or temperature in arctic regions.

6. Have students create a "What if . . ." book or bulletin board showing imaginative use of variables, such as the zebra losing its stripes or a cactus shedding its spines.

From *Living with the Land*, Copyright © 1998 Good Year Books.

EXPERIMENT RECORD SHEET: VARIABLES AND CONSTANTS

Group Members _____

EXPERIMENT NUMBER 1

Our constants will be _____ .

Our variables will be_____

We predict the following results:

_____

_____

_____

Our actual results were:

_____

_____

_____

EXPERIMENT NUMBER 2

Our constants will be _____ .

Our variables will be_____ .

We predict the following results:

_____

_____

_____

Our actual results were:

_____

_____

_____

PHARAOH'S LOST TOMB

OBJECTIVE

The purpose of this lesson is to provide practice for students in the use of the compass rose and reference points.

PROCEDURE

1. Ask the students to pretend that, like Hansel and Gretel, they are lost in the woods. Instead of dropping bread crumbs, they've stashed a compass in one of their back pockets. How will this help them find the way home?

2. Review cardinal directions (N, S, E, and W) and intermediate directions (NE, SE, SW, and NW) with the class. Review the concept of reference point using a stationary object in the classroom, such as a chalkboard. (For example: What direction is Kay's desk from the chalkboard?)

3. Have students work in pairs to create three questions about reference points using a stationary object in the classroom. Have them exchange questions with another pair and answer the questions they receive.

4. Ask students to complete the worksheet individually or in pairs and to check the completed map with other students.

EXTENSIONS

1. Ask students to write a fractured version of "Hansel and Gretel." Tell them to make changes so that the story is more humorous.

2. Create an archaeology dig by having students glue small, inexpensive trinkets to the bottom of a small box, such as a shoe box. They write directions for a classmate to "discover" the treasure, making their directions similar to those on the worksheet. Then they should cover the items with sand, exchange boxes, and go exploring. Make sure students provide a starting point.

3. Have students make maps of their routes from school to home.

4. Have students research the treasure buried with King Tut.

5. Have students make a cutaway diagram of an Egyptian pyramid.

PHARAOH'S LOST TOMB

Name(s) _____

Finding your way around a desert can be difficult. Knowing how to use a compass might help you survive—or find a great treasure!

In the space below, draw a compass rose, showing cardinal and intermediate directions.

Use the compass rose and the secret directions below to help you draw the map to the pharaoh's lost tomb. Draw your symbols on a separate piece of paper. Use a ruler. Keep the written directions and your symbol map in different locations to make it harder for bandits to find the treasure if you're ambushed along the way.

SECRET DIRECTIONS

KEY: 10 km = 1 cm

Put your ruler lengthwise along the top edge of the paper, which will be the northern part of your map. Starting in the left-hand corner of the paper, go 30 km (3 cm) E, and put a dot. This is your first reference point. From the dot, go 50 km S and draw some mountains. Go 90 km SE, and draw a snake. Go 80 km S, and draw a palm tree. Go 100 km NW, and draw a sun. Go 170 km SE, and draw a scorpion. Go 120 km NW, and draw a crescent moon. Go 80 km E, and draw a star. Go 70 km N, and draw a pyramid. Dig down 2 m, and you will find the entrance to the pharaoh's lost tomb!

SAN OR TOURIST POINT OF VIEW

OBJECTIVE

The purpose of this lesson is for students to develop an appreciation for varying opinions about the Bushman of the Kalahari. They will use a graphic organizer to record their ideas.

PROCEDURE

1. Discuss different and exotic vacation locations. Explain that people are becoming more curious about remote areas of the world. Photographic safaris and rain-forest excursions have become popular. Travel agents are developing "ecotour" packages for clients.

2. Locate the Kalahari Desert on a map. Ask students why this region is popular with tourists. If needed, discuss characteristics of the Kalahari Desert.

3. Discuss the importance of the Kalahari in maintaining the traditional San, or Bushman, way of life. (Note: This group of people prefer to be called "San," but they are called "Bushman" in many resources.)

4. Explain that some San who have lived in the Kalahari for generations feel that the desert is their home and that tourists are not welcome. However, tourists feel that they have the right to explore the desert and that they are not harming the ecosystem.

5. Divide the students into cooperative groups of four. Tell the students that you are going to assign half the class to take on the role of the San and the other half to take on the role of tourists.

6. Tell the students to write down reasons to support the viewpoint of their people—the San or the tourists. Pass out a copy of the San or Tourist Point of View sheet to each group.

7. Allow the students fifteen minutes to work cooperatively.

8. Have the students share viewpoints and supporting details with the class.

EXTENSIONS

1. Have the students transfer their personal viewpoints into a letter written to a San or a tourist.

2. Have the students take on the opposing point of view and list reasons.

3. Allow the class to debate the merits of these or other points of view.

4. Brainstorm a list of possible resolutions to the conflict between the tourists and the San.

5. Do a similar activity with a Native American tribe and European settlers of a hundred years ago.

From *Living with the Land*, Copyright © 1998 Good Year Books.

SAN OR TOURIST POINT OF VIEW

Name(s) _____

We believe that we, the _____

belong on this land because . . .

_____

_____

_____

Reason 1 _____

_____

_____

Reason 2 _____

_____

_____

Reason 3 _____

_____

_____

Summarizing Statement _____

_____

_____

THE MIGHTY SAGUARO

OBJECTIVE

The purpose of this lesson is to have students use listening and note-taking skills to form an opinion about the saguaro cactus of the Sonoran Desert.

PROCEDURE

1. Discuss the importance of all living things in the environment.

2. Ask students to think of one plant or animal that is found only in your region. Discuss what would happen to animals, people, and the environment as a whole without this plant or animal.

3. Tell students about the unique cactus called *saguaro* that lives in the Sonoran Desert:

   - Found only in the Sonora Desert

   - Grows as tall as 50 feet

   - Lives 150 years

   - Provides homes to many animals when it is alive and after it dies. Some of these animals are the Gila woodpecker, elf owl, and Harris's hawk, as well as many insects.

   - Provides food to many animals. Some of these animals include the long-nosed bat, white-winged dove, coyote, and javelina, and many insects.

   - Tohono O'odham, a southwest Indian tribe, rely on the saguaro for food and tools.

5. Discuss the amount of time it takes a saguaro to grow and all of the predators it will have to face in that time.

6. Have the students fill out The Mighty Saguaro worksheet.

7. When everyone is finished, share the students' writing, and discuss again how important this cactus is to our environment.

EXTENSIONS

1. Create a bulletin board in your classroom of a saguaro. Have students place their worksheets around it.

2. Have the students write a paragraph from one predator's point of view.

3. Have the students draw the stages of life of a saguaro, from a seedling to the mighty giant it can become.

4. Have students draw and write about a living saguaro and a dead one. Ask them to compare the two.

THE MIGHTY SAGUARO

Name(s) _____

How can I survive? I am the mighty saguaro, and I can grow to be ten times as large as some of my predators, but I am defenseless against one dangerous predator. HELP! I can deal with flash floods, dry climate, and animal predators, but now . . . MAN! Human beings need to know me better.

Write the words to show the world how important I am to the desert ecosystem.

_____

_____

_____

_____

_____

_____

_____

_____

_____

_____

_____

THE FLYING STICK

From *Living with the Land*, Copyright © 1998 Good Year Books.

OBJECTIVE

This lesson introduces students to a game played by San (Bushman) children. The students will chart results of the game and create a bar graph.

PROCEDURE

1. Gather materials needed to play the game and create the graph:

   • Yardsticks and rulers

   • Sticks that are equivalent in size and shape, approximately 2 feet long and 2 inches wide in diameter

   • Graph paper

2. Tell the students that they are going to use their measuring skills while playing a game that San children have played for centuries. Explain that tribal games were both recreational and educational. This particular game sharpened hunting skills.

3. Divide students into groups of four.

4. Explain the rules of the game:

   • Each player throws the stick as far as he or she can.

   • Each player throws from the same spot, which is marked with a ruler.

   • The yardstick is used to measure the distance of each throw.

   • Each player has four turns.

5. The students need to record the distance of each throw on The Flying Stick chart. This data will later be used to create a graph.

6. Play the game outside. Monitor the measurements and record keeping throughout the game.

7. When all students have completed the game, explain that they are going to create a bar graph using the data gathered during the game. The graph should include

   • A title

   • Labeled vertical and horizontal axes

   • An accurate depiction of the results

8. Provide time for the groups to share and compare graphs.

THE FLYING STICK *(continued)*

EXTENSIONS

1. Create a class bar graph, combining the results of all the groups.

2. Have students create a line graph using the results.

3. Discuss the concept of probability with the students. Ask them these two questions:

   • Was the game fair?

   • How could you make the game fair or unfair?

4. Have the students convert their results from feet to inches and create a new graph.

5. Play the game using estimation. Have the students estimate the distances and then use actual measurements to compare the difference.

THE FLYING STICK

Name(s) _____

Record the results of your game using the following chart.

Players:

1. _____   3. _____

2. _____   4. _____

	Throw 1	Throw 2	Throw 3	Throw 4
Player 1				
Player 2				
Player 3				
Player 4				

WATER OF LIFE

From Living with the Land, Copyright © 1998 Good Year Books.

OBJECTIVE

The purpose of this project is for students to use various resources to research information about irrigation, take notes, and transform their notes into a calendar.

PROCEDURE

1. This project requires a week or more for research and construction of a calendar from notes. Schedule three days for research in the library or media center. Ask the media person in your building to help you copy blank calendars from a computer program and to find blank formats for captions and illustrations. Find out if a binding machine and binder strips are available for finishing calendars. You will need plenty of 8 1/2-by-11-inch construction paper on which to paste the completed calendars.

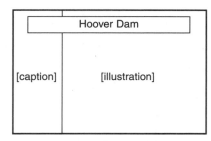

2. Discuss the concept of irrigation to determine prior knowledge. Give each student a copy of the Water of Life Web sheet. Using various resources, particularly encyclopedias, have students add detailed examples to each subcategory in the web. (One subcategory is blank for a topic they feel is not covered by the other subcategories.)

3. When this activity is completed, have students share and compare data. Explain to students that they are going to create an irrigation calendar. They should choose one main theme from their web notes. They must have twelve supporting examples for their theme. Pass out copies of the Irrigation Project Organizer sheet to each student. You can decide to have students work individually, in pairs, or in groups at this stage. Have students select a theme based on their web research and continue their research to see if they can find subtopics to support it. Students will need teacher guidance on an individual basis to expand or limit themes.

4. Pass out copies of the Irrigation Calendar Notes sheet (four per student). Remind students that notes consist of key words and phrases, not complete sentences. Note-taking space is limited to the boxes to reinforce this concept. Notes will be used to develop captions for the actual calendar.

5. When students have finished their notes, pass out copies of the blank calendar and of the blank formats for captions, if you have them. Give examples of how to construct captions from notes. Monitor student construction of illustrations and captions to make sure they stay on the topic. If you plan to grade this project, pass out copies of the Irrigation Calendar Project Checklist to students. Provide time for periodic peer conferencing so students may review and evaluate progress.

6. Have students sequence and paste their completed calendars on oaktag. Get the calendars bound for a professional look; or staple them or punch holes and tie them with string. Punch a hole in the top center of each page to hang the calendars.

7. Provide time for students to share their calendars. Evaluate with the class the pluses and minuses of calendar production.

EXTENSIONS

1. Modify the project to research desert people, locations, plants, or animals.

2. Make a blank copy of a world map, and mark the location of major dam systems.

3. Build a working model of an irrigation system.

4. Write to a calendar company requesting information on how to submit calendar theme ideas.

5. Use a favorite illustration and caption to create a T-shirt design.

WATER OF LIFE WEB SHEET

Name(s) _____

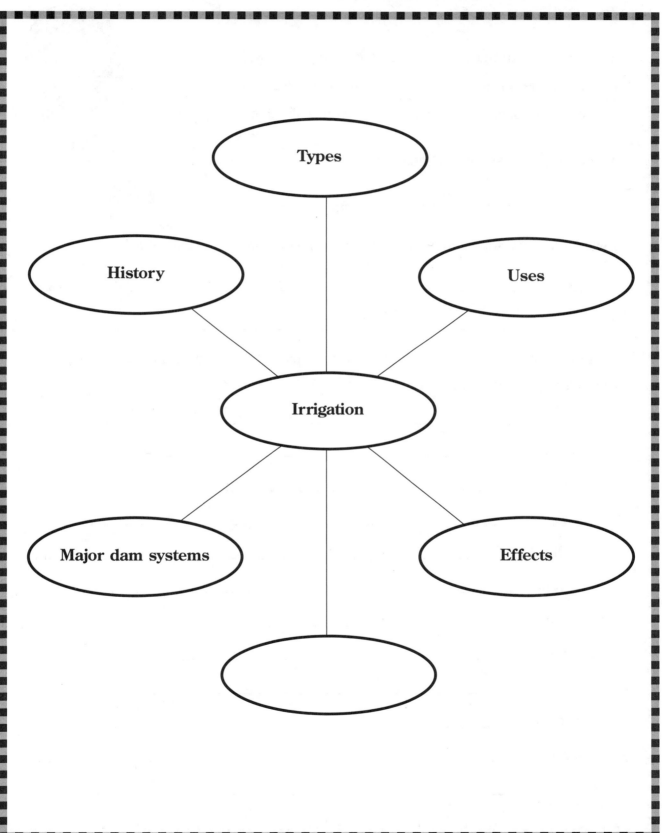

IRRIGATION PROJECT ORGANIZER

Name _____ Due Date_____

You are going to make an irrigation calendar. You will pick a theme, create illustrations, and write detailed captions to explain each illustration on your calendar.

The theme I chose for my calendar is

_____ .

I will look in the following sources to find information for my calendar.

_____

_____

Write a summary, in note form, of what the topic will be for each month to support the theme you selected.

January _____

February _____

March _____

April _____

May _____

June _____

July _____

August _____

September _____

October _____

November _____

December _____

IRRIGATION CALENDAR NOTES

Name _____ Theme _____

The Topic _____

The Topic _____

The Topic _____

REMEMBER: Notes are words and phrases about the subtopic. They are short, not complete sentences. Abbreviations are OK, and notes should stay on topic.

IRRIGATION CALENDAR PROJECT CHECKLIST

Name _____ Due Date_____

This sheet, and all the materials listed, must be handed in with your calendar.

RESEARCH (30 points)

_____ Project organizer: list of theme and monthly subtopics

_____ Notes packet: key words and phrases related to topics

_____ Bibliography: entries in standard format, recorded on back of notes packet

PRODUCT (50 points)

_____ Topic captions: summary or description of research written in your own words

_____ Illustrations: supports topic captions

_____ Cover: theme title, author/illustrator

PRESENTATION (20 points)

_____ Mechanics: spelling, capitalization, punctuation, and so on

_____ Neatness

Teacher Comments:

Grade:

From *Living with the Land*, Copyright © 1998 Good Year Books.

DESERT GLOSSARY

Name(s) _____

Bedouin: A tribe that lives in the Sahara Desert and herds animals.

Bushman [San]: A tribe that lives in the Kalahari Desert and gathers food.

Caravan: A group traveling in the desert that stays together for protection.

Culture: Peoples' way of life, including food, shelter, work, clothing, laws, language, transportation, and arts.

Desalination: A way of turning salt water into fresh water.

Desert: Land that gets less than 10 inches of precipitation a year.

Desertification: The growth or spreading of desert regions.

Dormant: In a state of rest; inactive.

Drought: A long period of time with no precipitation.

Erosion: The wearing away of land by wind or rain.

Evaporation: When heat causes water to change to water vapor.

Irrigation: Man-made canals, sprinklers, or other systems that bring water to crops.

Kalahari: A desert in southern Africa.

Mining: Taking minerals from the earth.

Mirage: A desert illusion caused by sun and heat.

Nomads: People who move from place to place, searching for food and water.

Oasis: A place in the desert where water is found.

Saguaro: A tall cactus that stores water for long periods.

Sahara: The largest desert in the world, in northern Africa.

Sonora Desert: A large desert in the southwestern United States.

Succulent: A plant that stores water in its body, such as a cactus.

Transpiration: Plant sweat; desert plants adapt to conserve moisture.

RAIN-FOREST REGIONS

By definition, rain forests are places that receive 80 or more inches of rain annually. There are many types of rain forests, such as temperate or montane, but the most prominent is the tropical rain forest. Tropical rain forests are found between the Tropic of Cancer and the Tropic of Capricorn. The largest rain forests of this type are the Amazon Basin in South America and the Congo in Africa.

The climate in tropical rain forests remains warm and constant all year. Showers occur almost daily. Vegetation is dense and layered. Trees form a thick canopy. Their branches are home to plants such as epiphytes and bromeliads. These plants in turn provide food and shelter for birds, insects, and small animals. In the understory, woody vines, called *lianas,* wind their way among tree trunks. Some plants on the forest floor grow 20 feet tall with fronds up to 6 feet long.

Tropical rain forests are sometimes called jungles. They cover less than one-sixth of the Earth's land surface, yet 75 percent of all known species of plants and animals are found in tropical rain forests. Many of these species are becoming extinct before they have been identified by scientists. Much of the world's oxygen is produced by the plants in these regions.

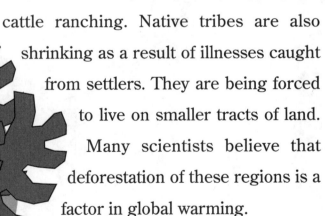

Tropical rain forests have been severely cut back by logging and cattle ranching. Native tribes are also shrinking as a result of illnesses caught from settlers. They are being forced to live on smaller tracts of land. Many scientists believe that deforestation of these regions is a factor in global warming.

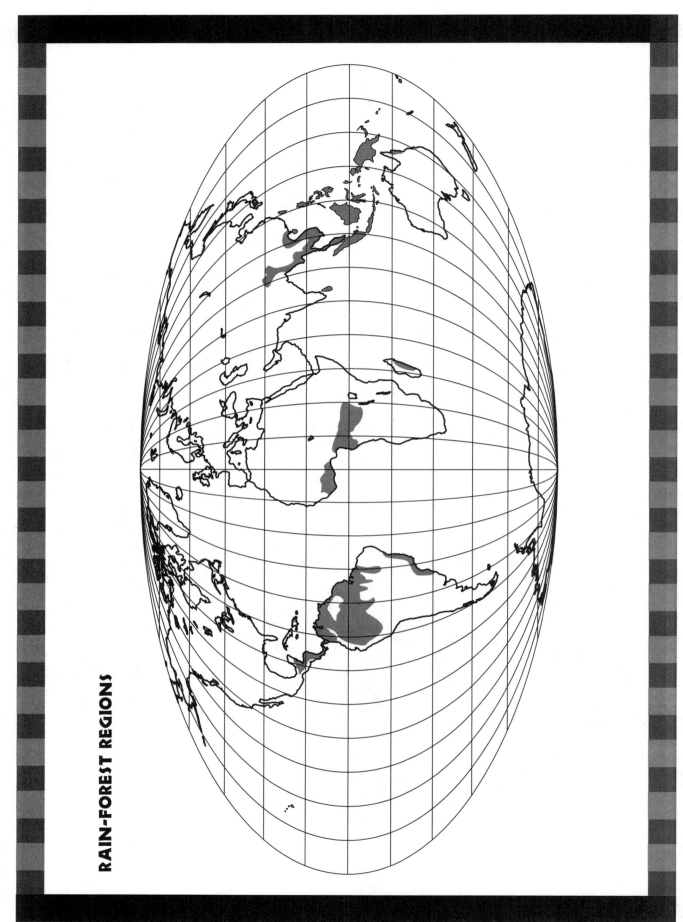

RAIN-FOREST REGIONS

RAIN-FOREST MOBILE RESEARCH

OBJECTIVE

The purpose of this lesson is for students to research specific rain-forest communities and their food chains. The students will then present their findings to the class. This lesson follows an introduction to the rain-forest environment.

PROCEDURE

1. Gather materials needed for making mobiles, such as hangers, dowels, markers, and paper. Make arrangements to take your class to the library or media center to do research, or sign out materials for students to use in class.

2. Discuss the concept of community and how all living things interact with one another through relationships. List the following relationships on the board, and have students give examples for each category:

   producer *(plants)*
   consumer *(animals)*
   predator *(eats other animals)*
   prey *(hunted by other animals)*
   parasite *(feeds on living things; is harmful)*
   host *(harmed by parasite)*
   symbiosis *(when two or more living things benefit from relationship)*

3. Discuss the concept of food chains, explaining how one animal may be both predator and prey. For example, a snake will eat frogs and an eagle will eat snakes. Some categories will have longer lists than others.

4. Form groups, and assign each a category to research, such as:

   Plants
   Mammals
   Birds
   Reptiles
   Amphibians
   Fish

5. Provide each student with a copy of the Rain-Forest Mobile Research Notes sheet. Each member of the group must choose a different item to research within the assigned category. Remind students to stay on the topic and to focus only on the information requested on the sheet. Have each group discuss the overall construction of their mobile before they conduct individual research.

6. Have the groups create mobiles using the information gathered from the research sheets. Provide time for students to practice presenting the information on the mobiles before calling on them to share with the class. Hang the finished mobiles from the classroom ceiling to display them.

EXTENSIONS

1. Have the students write a letter to the president of the United States explaining the effect the destruction of the rain forest has on relationships within that community.

2. Have the students create a rain-forest relationships book and read it to someone in a lower grade.

3. Ask students to compare the relationships found in the rain forest to those of a different region, such as the desert.

4. Brainstorm a list of people with whom students have positive relationships. Students should chose a specific person to write about and should share the piece with that individual.

5. Have the class make three-dimensional models of the items researched and display them in the library or media center.

RAIN-FOREST MOBILE RESEARCH NOTES

Group Member _____

Our group's category is _____

Topic that I will research in this category is _____

General Description (include size, color, etc.):

_____

_____

Type of relationship in community:

_____

_____

How nutrients are obtained:

_____

_____

Fascinating or unusual facts:

_____

_____

The caption of my illustration will be:

_____

_____

I will help my group present by:

_____

_____

This is a hard nut to crack.

THE GREAT KAPOK TREE

OBJECTIVE

The purpose of this lesson is to have students understand the importance of trees in the ecosystem of the rain forest and to explore the effects of deforestation. Students will compare and contrast the environment when the kapok tree is present with the environment and when there are no kapok tress.

PROCEDURE

1. Have the students list the many varied and unusual things found in the rain forest.

2. Discuss how each listed item helps preserve the rain-forest ecosystem.

3. Analyze the cover of the book *The Great Kapok Tree* by Lynne Cherry. Ask the students how and why the kapok tree is important to the ecosystem of the rain forest.

4. Read the book to the students, and discuss the kapok tree's role in the ecosystem.

5. Group students in pairs and pass out copies of the worksheet that follows. Share pictures and insights when finished.

EXTENSIONS

1. Ask students to imagine a major change in their environment, such as the school burns down. Have students list ways this event would affect their lives.

2. Make a T-chart listing similarities and differences between the ecosystems of the rain forest and the desert.

3. Have students research spices that come from rain forests. Collect samples in plastic bags, and label them. Find a large bare branch that has fallen off a tree, attach it to a bulletin board, and hang the samples on it to enjoy a "spice tree."

THE GREAT KAPOK TREE

Name(s) _____

1. Draw two pictures of the rain forest, one with the kapok tree and one without the kapok tree.

 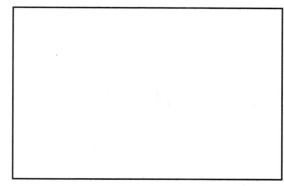

2. For each picture, list two things that are *similar.*

   WITH   **WITHOUT**

   _____   _____

   _____   _____

3. For each picture, list two things that are *different.*

   WITH   **WITHOUT**

   _____   _____

   _____   _____

ADVANCE WARNING

The purpose of this lesson is for students to preread nonfiction material about the greenhouse effect and to process the material in diagram form. The prereading strategy used taps into prior vocabulary knowledge. It also "tunes students in" to the selection they will read. This strategy is helpful when having students read technical information.

PROCEDURE

1. Before you begin, collect diagrams—particularly diagrams that show ecological or other cycles—from newspapers and magazines. Also ask students to bring them in.

2. Put the following words on the board:

    infrared   **atmosphere**   **greenhouse**
    radiate   **pollution**   **carbon dioxide**

    Discuss each word individually. Solicit definitions or associations that come to the students' minds.

3. Tell students that they will be reading an article about the greenhouse effect. Pass out copies of The Greenhouse Effect worksheet. Have the students work individually, in pairs, or in groups. Tell students to highlight words that were listed on the board before they read the selection and to draw the diagram. The diagram should be similar to the one shown at the right.

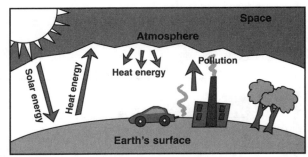

EXTENSIONS

1. Arrange a class trip to a local greenhouse to learn how it operates.

2. Create a classroom terrarium using mosses and small plants. Compare the amount of water the terrarium needs with the amount needed by plants grown outdoors.

3. Have students design posters to save the rain forests.

4. Have students investigate the effects of pollution on the water cycle.

From *Living with the Land*, Copyright © 1998 Good Year Books.

THE GREENHOUSE EFFECT

Name(s) _____

Directions: Read the article below. Draw a diagram showing the greenhouse effect and what has caused it to change over the last hundred years.

HEATING UP THE GREENHOUSE

The sun in our solar system is a powerful source of heat and light energy. The sun's energy penetrates Earth's atmosphere, which is a layer of gases surrounding our planet. Solar energy warms the surface of the Earth, creating infrared, or heat energy. Some gases in the atmosphere, primarily carbon dioxide and water vapor, absorb this heat energy and radiate it back towards the Earth's surface. This natural phenomenon, known as the greenhouse effect, maintains a comfortable temperature that supports life. The processes of photosynthesis by plants and respiration by animals keep the amount of carbon dioxide in the atmosphere stable.

During the past century, the amount of carbon dioxide and other greenhouse gases in our atmosphere has been increasing. Pollution from factories and machines has dirtied the atmosphere. Burning millions of acres of rain forest also has increased the amount of greenhouse gases. As a result of the increase in greenhouse gases, more infrared energy is radiated back to the Earth's surface. Pollution causes less heat to escape into space. The temperature of the air and the Earth's surface increase.

GLOBAL ALERT!

OBJECTIVE

The purpose of this lesson is for students to explore the global effects of pollution, deforestation, and other environmental changes and to publish their findings in a newspaper article.

PROCEDURE

1. Ask students to bring in newspaper articles about the environment for two weeks prior to beginning this lesson. Gather a number of sources with up-to-date information on the topics listed in 3, below.

2. Review the concepts of global warming and the greenhouse effect. (See previous lesson, Advance Warning.) Review the elements of a newspaper article using the samples brought in by students. A newspaper article should:

    • Stick to the facts.

    • Stay on topic.

    • Answer the questions *who, what, when, where, why,* and *how.*

    • Be brief but informative.

3. Explain to the students that they will be writing a class newspaper about Earth's changing environment. They will be using all available resources to research their topic. Set up groups and assign each group one of the following topics:

deforestation	**air pollution**
global warming	**water pollution**
melting polar icecaps	**land pollution**
desertification	

4. If possible, reserve time for the class to work in the school computer lab. Students can research topics on the Internet and use a software publishing program for final publication. Groups should draft their reports on the Global Alert! worksheet and edit and revise with peers before submitting the articles for publication.

5. Make copies of the newspaper for each student. Make extra copies for the school office, library, or media center.

From *Living with the Land,* Copyright © 1998 Good Year Books.

GLOBAL ALERT! *(continued)*

EXTENSIONS

1. Obtain permission to sell copies of the newspaper in the lunchroom or school store. Send the profits to an environmental group or "adopt" a whale, a section of a rain forest, or a coral reef.

2. Create ads from environmental groups for the newspaper.

3. Invite a local newspaper editor to discuss modern publication methods.

4. E-mail copies of the newspaper to other schools or to environmental groups.

5. Have students research environmental situations and create news reports. Videotape their reports to share with other classes.

GLOBAL ALERT!

Group Members _____

Our newspaper article will be about

_____

Four important facts readers should know about this topic are

1. _____

2. _____

3. _____

4. _____

In the space below, write a rough draft of your article
and create a drawing for the newspaper.

Headline

Drawing

Caption

Earth Colony Established on Mars!

From *Living with the Land*, Copyright © 1998 Good Year Books.

YOU ARE WHAT YOU EAT

OBJECTIVE

The purpose of this lesson is for students to investigate and learn about the role of vitamins and minerals in a nutritious diet by studying tropical diseases and rain-forest cures.

PROCEDURE

1. Students will need to consult encyclopedias to complete this lesson. Additional resources, such as books on human nutrition, are helpful aids.

2. Write the following questions on the board:
   - What are vitamins and minerals?
   - Where do they come from?
   - Why are they important?

   Have the class brainstorm possible answers and list them on the board. Keep the answers on the board so that you can add more when students finish the worksheet.

3. Set up research groups and distribute copies of the worksheet You Are What You Eat. Provide research leads if necessary. Monitor research for accuracy.

4. When students have completed the worksheet, review the data on the board. Using notes from the worksheet, students should provide additional answers.

5. Discuss benefits of sharing and checking notes with classmates. Were students able to add specific information to support their original ideas? Why?

EXTENSIONS

1. Invite the school nurse or cafeteria manager to talk to the class about proper nutrition.

2. Make a nutritional value chart, including categories such as fat, protein, calories, vitamins, and minerals. Have the class research the nutritional value of some healthy foods and some "junk" foods, and record results on the chart.

3. Ask students to pretend they are shipmates on a long voyage 250 years ago. Half will eat citrus fruit on a regular basis, and half will eat no citrus fruit. Review data on scurvy. Keep a health log where students record health descriptions from the point of view of a sailor. Students record entries as if they were entering them into the log at six-month intervals over a two-year period (total: four entries).

4. Have a rain-forest celebration breakfast where students bring in breakfast foods and salads made with ingredients that originated in rain-forest regions. Invite another class to share your feast.

YOU ARE WHAT YOU EAT

Researchers _____

Fruits and vegetables contain elements necessary for healthy nutrition. Some illnesses are directly related to deficiencies in essential vitamins and minerals.

Research two of the illnesses from the box below. Describe characteristics of the illness and correct treatment.

anemia	beriberi	goiter
pellagra	rickets	scurvy

ILLNESS	CHARACTERISTICS	TREATMENT

Many foods we eat originally came from rain forests. Choose one food from the list to research. Explain how this food contributes to a healthy diet.

banana	cashew	pepper	pineapple
lemon	avocado	papaya	

We chose to research _____. This food is important to a healthy

diet because _____

_____

_____

ATLAS FACT-FINDING MISSION

OBJECTIVE

The purpose of this lesson is for students to locate and interpret information from thematic maps and other geographic resources. Students use data gathered from research to create questions that will be answered by classmates.

PROCEDURE

1. Obtain at least one atlas for every two students. Pair up students in teams.

2. Review the purpose of an atlas. List suggestions on a chalkboard or overhead. Allow each team to peruse their atlas for five minutes and record additional uses. Possible examples are population patterns and land use.

3. Distribute a copy of the worksheet "Atlas Fact-Finding Mission" to each team. Discuss the land regions listed on the sheet, asking students to predict what information they expect to find for each category. Then have students begin the activity. Encourage students to be specific when researching and recording data. For example, under location, students should include the continent, compass direction, and latitude and longitude.

4. When students have completed their research, have them exchange sheets with another team and answer the questions on the sheet they receive. Compare the data recorded in the grids. Did all teams record data in the exact same words? Why?

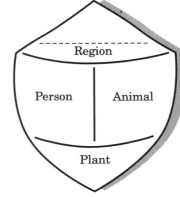

EXTENSIONS

1. Divide students into team, and have each team select a region from the worksheet. Using supplemental resources, students should create a shield for their region similar to the model at the right. Display projects on a bulletin board.

2. Use student-created questions to create an open-book atlas quiz.

3. Have a dress-up day where each team dresses appropriately for a region of their choice. Students must locate the region on a wall map and explain to peers the reasons for their choice of clothing.

4. Choose one subcategory, and create a graph using the regions on the worksheet.

ATLAS FACT-FINDING MISSION

Mission Specialists _____

DIRECTIONS

Use an atlas or other source to complete the chart below.

REGION	LOCATION	ANNUAL PRECIPITATION	TEMPERATURE RANGE	NATURAL RESOURCES
Gobi Desert				
Amazon Rain Forest				
Great Sandy Desert				
Glacier Bay				

Use the completed chart to answer the following questions.

1. What is the difference in temperature between the hottest and coldest region?

   _____

2. How many regions are in the Northern Hemisphere? _____

3. What is the difference in annual precipitation between the Gobi Desert and the

   Amazon rain forest? _____

4. Which region has the most natural resources? _____
   Write a sentence explaining your choice.

   _____

5. What is the latitude for the Great Sandy Desert? _____

Use the data from the chart to create three questions for another team to answer.

_____

_____

_____

From *Living with the Land*, Copyright © 1998 Good Year Books.

SOUTH AMERICAN CITIES

OBJECTIVES

The purpose of this lesson is for students to use map skills—particularly to use scale and to research facts about South American cities surrounding the Amazon region.

PROCEDURE

1. Gather research materials, including atlases and encyclopedias with information on South American cities. You may wish to obtain tour brochures from a travel agency. This project may be done individually, but it will be more interesting and make better use of resources if it is done in pairs or groups.

2. Using a wall map, review the estimated length and width of South America. Ask if any students have visited South America. What countries did they visit? What was the purpose of their trip? What did they see during their visit?

3. Review the use of scale, emphasizing rounding of distance, using locations on the wall map.

4. Tell students that they will plan an imaginary tour of South American cities. Encourage them to research information about the cities before planning their itinerary.

5. Set up groups. Pass out copies of the South American Cities worksheet to each group. Provide research leads if necessary.

6. When the worksheets are completed, allow time for groups to share their itineraries with the class.

EXTENSIONS

1. Ask the chamber of commerce of a nearby city to send a representative to speak to your class about the city.

2. Using maps and other resources, have the class plan a tour of your own city or town. Take a field trip following the tour they design.

3. Contact local travel agencies to find a travel agent or traveler who will speak to the class about his or her adventures in South America.

4. Have students design a travel poster promoting their favorite South American city.

5. Have each student design a postcard featuring a point of interest in a South American city. Display the postcards in an album or on a bulletin board.

SOUTH AMERICAN CITIES

Applicant(s) _____

Some South American cities are sponsoring a contest to promote tourism. They are giving away a 10,000-kilometer tour, including air transportation and hotel accommodations. Use an atlas or a map with scale to estimate the distances from city to city. Then complete the application below.

RULES

- You may start in any South American city listed on the map.

- Your entire tour must not exceed an estimated 10,000 km.

- On the basis of a unique feature of each city area, list a reason you chose this destination.

- Outline your tour route on the map.

CONTEST APPLICATION

DEPARTURE CITY	ARRIVAL CITY	DISTANCE TRAVELED	REASON FOR VISIT

From *Living with the Land*, Copyright © 1998 Good Year Books.

RAIN-FOREST FRACTIONS

The purpose of this lesson is for students to review operations using the following fraction concepts: lowest terms, equivalent fractions, improper fractions, and mixed numbers. The review of fraction concepts is based on mathematical word problems about the rain forest.

PROCEDURE

Worksheet Answers
1. 3 miles
2. 33.25; 142.5; 1,733.75 leaves
3. 5.25 hours
4. 46 sq. miles
5. 12/25
6. 12 species
7. 48 plants
8. 10 acres
9. 1/3
10. 5 hours

1. Tell students that 14/100 of the world was once rain forest. Ask students if this fraction is in lowest terms. Reduce it with the class.

2. Next tell the students that today, 7/100 of the world is rain forest. Ask what fraction of the earth's rain forest we have lost.

3. Tell students that today they will be solving rain-forest word problems that will review the following fraction concepts: lowest terms, mixed numbers, improper fractions. Review these concepts quickly with the class by working examples on the board.

4. Allow students time to work on the problems individually or with a partner.

5. Go over answers to the word problems.

EXTENSIONS

1. Ask students to collect recipes for trail mix or fruit salad. Choose a favorite recipe and convert the ingredients to make enough for the class. Have students bring in the ingredients, create the food, and consume the results of their work!

2. Have students find out how much of the earth is made up of desert, grassland, and mountain; translate the amounts into percentages, and make a circle graph.

3. Make a tally chart of the months in which students were born. Have students create fraction word problems using the data.

4. Ask students to keep track of time spent on after-school activities for a week. Set up categories in advance, such as homework, recreation, and sports. Have students compare the results with the amount of time spent in school each week.

5. Collect copies of a menu from a local restaurant for students to use in creating word problems using percentages. For example, what percentage of the entrees are fish dishes?

RAIN-FOREST FRACTIONS

Name(s) _____

DIRECTIONS

Answer the following word problems.

Don't forget to label your answers.

1. Some Yanamamo people are traveling through the Brazilian rain forest looking for a kapok tree. They have already traveled 2-3/4 miles. If they travel 1-1/4 mile more, how far will they have traveled? _____

2. A leaf-cutter ant eats four and three-quarters leaves a day. How many leaves will it eat in a week? _____ in a month? _____ in a year? _____

3. A Tupi spent 4-3/4 hours hunting. He also spent 2/4 of an hour gathering berries. How long did the Tupi spend hunting and gathering? _____

4. The rain forests of the world are being destroyed at the alarming rate of 115 square miles a day. If we reduced cutting the rain forest by 2/5, how many square miles would be saved each day? _____

5. Approximately 48 out of every 100 workers in Brazil are in the service industry. Write this fraction in its lowest terms. _____

6. The biodiversity of a rain forest is high. A botanist counted 60 different species of trees on one acre of land in the rain forest. An acre near his home in the United States has one-fifth that amount. How many species is that? _____

7. The botanist counted 64 epiphytes on a tree in the rain forest. Two-eighths of them were orchids. How many plants were not orchids? _____

8. Modern machinery can clear an acre of trees in 1-1/4 hours. How many acres can a logging company clear in a regular eight-hour workday? _____

9. There were 36 natives living in a village. Twenty-four of them were infected with malaria. In lowest terms, what fraction of the tribe was not infected? _____ ___

10. A Tupi child spent one-third of her day sleeping, two-sixths of it working, and one-eighth of it eating. How many hours did she have left for other activities? _____

From *Living with the Land*, Copyright © 1998 Good Year Books.

TURN IT AROUND

OBJECTIVE

The purpose of this lesson is to review antonyms and parts of speech, using a diamonte poem.

PROCEDURE

1. Diamonte is a form of poetry that starts out describing one thing and ends by describing its opposite. Like many forms of poetry, it has a specific format. Below are the format requirements for each line of the poem and an example.

1. Item or feeling to be described (item 1).	**Sun**
2. Two adjectives describing item 1.	**Yellow, hot,**
3. Three participles describing item 1.	**Scorching, blinding, evaporating,**
4. Four nouns: two describing item 1, two describing item 2.	**Flares, sunsets, craters, faces,**
5. Three participles describing item 2.	**Reflecting, changing, orbiting,**
6. Two adjectives describing item 2.	**Blue, romantic,**
7. Opposite item or feeling to be described (item 2).	**Moon**

2. Create a couple of these poems on your own before introducing them to the class. Collect resource books from your library or media center on rain forests, deserts, plains, and arctic climates.

3. Review the concept of antonyms, or opposites, with the class. Have students generate pairs and list them on the board. Set up groups.

4. Allow students time to review books, asking them to focus on the different climates they have been studying. Have them make lists of opposites they observe. Put this second list of pairs on chart paper or an overhead transparency.

5. Introduce the format for diamonte poetry, and work out two examples from the first list with the class.

6. Have each group take a pair of words from the second list and write their own diamonte to share with the class.

EXTENSIONS

1. Ask students to use the word pairs to create comic-strip-format dialogue between the objects.

2. Have students compare the two objects using a Venn diagram that focuses on similarities and differences.

3. Have students use a software program to write a "get well" card to a region under study. Ask them to focus on what they as individuals can do to help the region get better.

4. Ask students to research a tribe from an assigned region and to draw an picture of a tool used by the tribe. Compare the similarities and differences with the class.

PEOPLE OF THE RAIN FOREST

From *Living with the Land*, Copyright © 1998 Good Year Books.

OBJECTIVES

The purpose of this lesson is for students to research an Amazon tribe and to use data to creatively solve the tribe's financial problems.

PROCEDURE

1. Students need encyclopedias and other reference material relating to the tribes listed on the worksheet. (NOTE: Information about some tribes may not be easily found.) Set up research groups.

2. Ask students what they know about native tribes living in the Amazon region. Explain that anthropologists have lived with tribes in this region to study their cultures.

3. Review problem-solving strategies with the class. Explain that in the first stage, brainstorming, all answers are accepted without judgment. In the second stage, setting criteria, they must look at the requirements set by the tribe. They will use their criteria to eliminate or retain options. In the third stage, prioritizing, the group will evaluate and rank options from best to worst.

4. Pass out copies of the worksheet for People of the Rain Forest and monitor group interaction.

5. When students have completed the worksheets, have groups share their reports. Compare strategies used by different groups.

EXTENSIONS

1. Ask students to compare the recent history of Amazon tribes with that of Native American tribes in the late nineteenth century.

2. Have students research Chico Mendes, a famous rubber-tapper of South America, and make a picture book about his life.

3. Ask students to write a letter to a company that speaks out on environmental issues, such as Ben and Jerry's, asking for an explanation of how they use renewable rain-forest materials in their products.

4. Have students research the tagua nut, which is a renewable rain-forest product, and make a poster showing modern uses.

5. Ask students to apply problem-solving strategies to address a local issue that will affect them.

PEOPLE OF THE RAIN FOREST

Anthropology Team _____

Anthropologists study the development of human cultures around the world. Your anthropology team has been asked to do some research on Amazon tribes. Tribal leaders want you to recommend ways their tribe can make money to maintain their independence without harming the environment.

Choose one of the tribes below to research.
Record your notes in the boxes.

TRIBES

Tupi	Kayapo	Yanamamo
Bororo	Campa	Amahuaca
Tukano	Wyana	

TRIBE	ENVIRONMENT	FOOD SOURCES	CUSTOMS

On a separate piece of paper, problem solve by brainstorming, setting criteria, and prioritizing before you write your report.

ANTHROPOLOGISTS' REPORT

Based on our research of the _____ tribe, we make the following recom-
mendations as possible ways to help the tribe become more financially independent.

_____

_____

From *Living with the Land*, Copyright © 1998 Good Year Books.

RAIN-FOREST GLOSSARY

Name(s) _____

Amazon River: The largest river in South America; flows through Brazil.

Canopy: The thick layer of leaves and branches that blocks sunlight to the forest floor below.

Climate: The weather in a place over a long period of time.

Consumer: A living thing that gets energy by eating other living things.

Decomposer: A living thing that breaks down dead plants and animals.

Ecosystem: A place where living and nonliving things affect one another.

Elevation: The height of land above sea level.

Emergents: Trees that stick out above the canopy.

Environment: Everything that surrounds and affects a living thing.

Epiphyte: A plant, such as an orchid, that lives on another plant but doesn't take its food from its host.

Forest floor: The lowest level of a rain forest.

Host: A living thing that is harmed by a parasite.

Liana: A common woody vine that grows in rain forests.

Mouth: The place where a river empties into a larger body of water.

Natives: Members of tribes that have lived in the Amazon Basin for thousands of years, such as the Tupi and Yanamamo.

Nutrients: Minerals that provide food for plants and animals when dissolved in water.

Parasite: A living thing that feeds on and harms another living thing.

Predator: An animal that hunts other animals.

Prey: An animal that is hunted.

Rain forest: Woodland that receives over 80 inches of rain per year.

Symbiosis: Relationship between two or more organisms that live closely together and benefit each other.

Tributary: A smaller river that flows into a larger one.

Understory: The layer of the rain forest between the forest floor and the canopy.

Yanomamo: A fierce native tribe that lives in the Amazon region.

ARCTIC
REGIONS

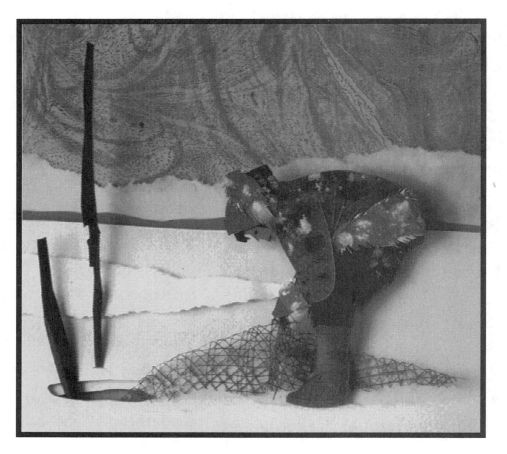

The Arctic region surrounds the frozen North Pole. The Arctic is generally defined as the area within the Arctic Circle, 66-1/2 degrees north latitude. The Arctic Circle includes the entire Arctic Ocean plus parts of North America, Greenland, and Europe and Asia.

The climate in the Arctic is cold and dry, and the region usually receives 10 inches or less of precipitation, mostly in the form of snow. Temperatures in the long, dark winter stay well below freezing. In the summer, even in areas where the sun never sets, temperatures stay cool, around 50 degrees Fahrenheit, due to the slanting rays of the sun.

The land in the northern regions is called *tundra*. It is a mostly flat, treeless area covered with lichens, grasses, and sedge. Permanently frozen soil, called *permafrost*, prevents the growth of forests. Numerous birds and mammals, such as reindeer and caribou, flourish during the summer. The plankton-rich waters of the Arctic Ocean are good feeding grounds for whales, seals, and birds.

Despite the harsh climate, native people, such as the Inuit and Lapps, have survived in the Arctic for thousands of years. Arctic mammals and fish are a staple of their diet. Most live differently today than did their ancestors, taking advantage of such modern technology as snowmobiles and computers to enhance their daily lives.

The two polar regions, the Arctic and Antarctic, are similar. Both are dry and frigid and are subject to strong winds. In both, there are areas of permanent ice. Only small plants survive. The oceans are thick with life.

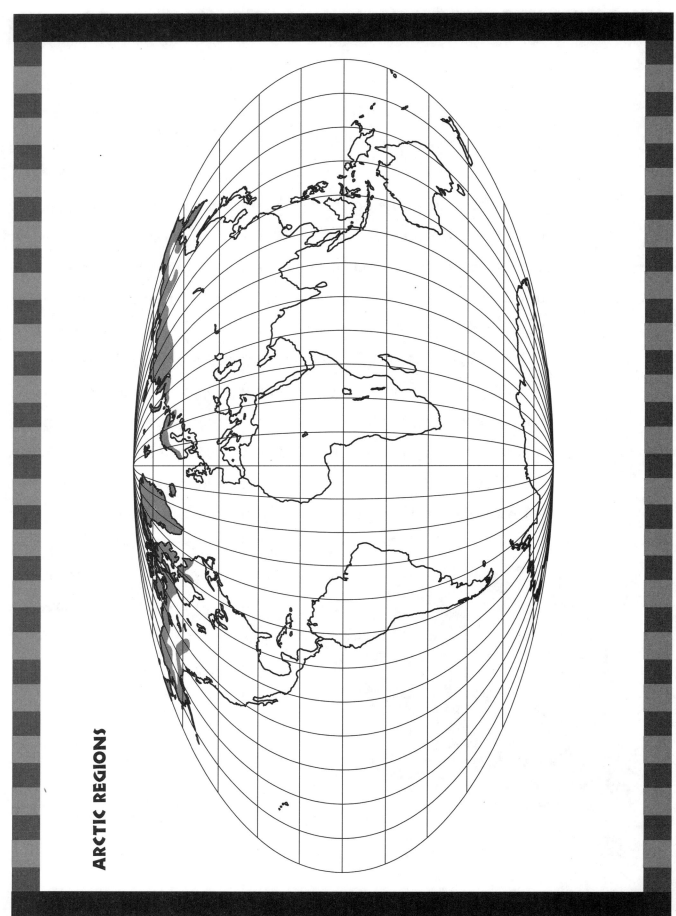

From *Living with the Land*, Copyright © 1998 Good Year Books.

A PICTURE IS WORTH A THOUSAND WORDS

This lesson is a prereading activity to introduce students to a nonfiction book about the Arctic. Students will practice inferring information.

PROCEDURE

1. Obtain multiple copies of a nonfiction book about the Arctic. If this is not possible, select a variety of illustrated books about the Arctic and modify the lesson.

2. Discuss with students how authors imply setting or feelings. Read aloud an example from a book students have been using in class. Ask students if it is possible to make inferences from a picture.

3. Present a picture from the book about the Arctic. Ask students to describe what they see. Encourage them to infer characteristics about the Arctic from the pictures. For example, the amount of snow and ice indicates cold temperatures.

4. Have the class discuss the book cover. What information can be inferred from the picture and the title? Model note-taking strategies on the chalkboard or on an overhead projector.

5. Tell the students that they are now going to learn from a nonfiction book about the Arctic. However, they are not going to have to read a single word. They will only have to look at the pictures.

6. Assign each child or group of children a picture in the book to study. Have them write notes to record what they infer from studying the picture. Explain that they will use their notes to talk to the class for one minute about their picture.

7. Allow each student or group one minute to present their inferences.

8. Summarize what the class learned about the Arctic from the pictures.

9. Read the book together, or assign the book to be read individually by the students.

A PICTURE IS WORTH A THOUSAND WORDS *(continued)*

EXTENSIONS

1. Do additional prereading activities with the students. Go over boldfaced and italicized words in the text.

2. Allow the students to bring in a desert, rain-forest, or plains photograph from home and talk about it for a minute.

3. Have the students design Arctic postcards, and display them on a bulletin board.

4. Ask students to pick a favorite chapter from a book with an illustrated cover. What can they infer from the picture? Have students decide on something else they want the cover to imply, and have them redesign the cover.

5. Cut scenes from old calendars. Ask students to take notes about the scenes and to use the notes to write poems. Post the scenes and the poems on a bulletin board.

IGLOO BLUEPRINT

The purpose of this lesson is to apply prior learning about geometry, measurement, and fractions to create an Inuit's blueprint for an igloo.

PROCEDURE

1. Collect samples of blueprints from a local architect.

2. Share and review the blueprints with the students, emphasizing the use of scale and other elements.

3. Review the terms *circle, diameter,* and *radius*. Also review fractions.

4. Tell students that they are going to apply their knowledge of fractions and parts of a circle to draw a blueprint for an Inuit igloo.

5. Review directions on the Igloo Blueprint handout and allow students time to complete it.

    Note: The diameter of the student's igloo should be 10 centimeters, and the entryway equal to 5 centimeters. Student drawings should have all of the elements shown below.

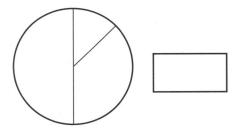

EXTENSIONS

1. Have students write a story to go along with one of the blueprints you provided.

2. Have the students write a skit about a typical day in an Inuit igloo.

3. Ask students to create their own math stories for other students to illustrate.

4. Have students create a life-sized igloo out of Styrofoam.

IGLOO BLUEPRINT

Name(s) _____

DIRECTIONS

Read the information below. Use the information to draw a blueprint of the inside of an igloo on a separate sheet of paper. Label each section. Add some interesting details. Pay close attention to measurement.

Please note: 1 cm = 1 ft

- An igloo is a small, temporary winter home for the Inuits of the Arctic. Igloos are made from blocks of ice to provide shelter on hunting trips.

- The interior area of an igloo is 10 feet in diameter. Half the space is used for sleeping on sealskin pads. This space is also used for sharing stories, cleaning harpoons, and discussing the day of hunting.

- Two-thirds of the remaining space is devoted to storing tools and hunting equipment, and one-sixth of the area is used for cooking. Inuits use small stoves to make tea and heat food.

- The Arctic environment is so cold that the Inuit often build an underground tunnel to the igloo. In length, the tunnel is equal to the radius of the igloo. It reduces the effects of frigid winds and also serves as a freezer, preserving carcasses and protecting them from scavengers.

ARCTIC ALLITERATION

OBJECTIVE

The purpose of this lesson is to expose students to a variety of arctic animals, to review parts of speech, and to have students create alliterative sentences.

PROCEDURE

1. Gather a variety of materials students can use to look up information about arctic animals. Each group will need a 4-by-6-inch index card.

2. Divide students into groups, and ask them to search for data on the Arctic. Brainstorm with the class a list of animals that live in arctic regions.

3. Review the parts of speech, particularly nouns, verbs, adjectives, and adverbs. Review the concept of alliteration, where most words in a sentence begin with similar sounds. An example is: "Lazy lizards lounge under lily leaves."

4. Give each group a copy of the Arctic Alliteration worksheet. Have them choose two animals to research, focusing on appearance and behavior. When they complete the worksheet, the group should write one of their alliterative sentences on the index card and should draw a picture to illustrate it. Each group should share the sentence and display the card on a bulletin board.

EXTENSIONS

1. Have students collect boxes of the same size and paste the illustrated sentences to the bottoms of the boxes. Build an "illuminating igloo" that tells about arctic animals.

2. Have students make a map of the Arctic, with a color-coded key to show the habitats of the animals researched.

3. Ask students to choose one animal, such as a polar bear, and research the ways the animal has adapted to a frigid environment.

4. Many animals have thick layers of blubber to protect them from the cold. Using two milk cartons of the same size, have students insulate one with Styrofoam or foam rubber, fill both with water, place them in a freezer, and observe how long each one takes to freeze.

ARCTIC ALLITERATION

Group Members _____

DIRECTIONS

1. Choose two arctic animals to write about.

2. Using available sources, look for words and phrases to describe the appearance and behavior of each animal, and record your notes in the boxes below.

3. Use your notes to write two alliterative sentences. Be creative!

4. Choose your favorite sentence to write on the index card and illustrate.

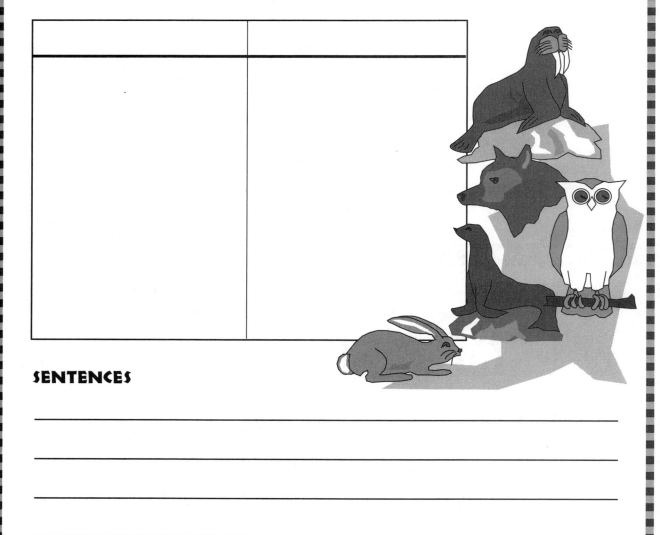

SENTENCES

_____

_____

_____

_____

PERISHABLE PEAS

OBJECTIVE

The purpose of this lesson is for students to use scientific methods to explore the effects of frigid polar temperatures on perishable items. Students collect, record, and report data.

PROCEDURE

1. Collect the following materials:

    • 2 locking-seal plastic sandwich bags per student

    • 1 thermometer per student

    • Masking tape or labels for each bag

    • Copies of the Perishable Peas Record Sheet

2. Ask students to bring in two fresh vegetables or fruits, such as peas, berries, or herbs.

3. Show students where the Arctic Circle is on a globe. Explain that winter temperatures in this region reach 50 degrees below zero or lower. Explain the term *perishable*. What effect would arctic temperatures have on perishable items? Can these low temperatures help people and animals living in the region? How?

4. Explain to students that they will conduct a long-term experiment to observe how temperature affects perishable items. Discuss how scientists use the process of hypothesis and experimentation to reach conclusions.

5. If students have brought in large fruits or vegetables, like oranges, cut them into sections. Have each student mark his or her name and the date on masking tape or labels attached to the bags. Place similarly sized pieces of produce in each bag.

6. Each student should have two bags. One will be kept on a shelf in the classroom. The student should take the other bag home and place it in the freezer.

7. Give each student a copy of the record sheet and have them punch holes in their sheets and keep them in their binder. Students should look at their fruits or vegetables and record observations every four days, paying close attention to changes in color and texture.

PERISHABLE PEAS *(continued)*

8. At the end of sixteen days, the class should share observations. Were notes detailed and accurate? What generalizations were made about the effects of temperature on perishable items? What were some unexpected results?

EXTENSIONS

1. Ask students to write a news report describing the effects on their community of a power outage lasting a week.

2. Have the class write a business letter to major frozen-food companies, such as Bird's-Eye or Sara Lee, asking for the company's history.

3. Have students research how people kept food fresh prior to the availability of electricity.

4. Ask students to research how the arctic fox and other animals living in polar regions use the natural refrigeration provided by frigid arctic temperatures.

5. Contact the produce manager of a food store in your area. Arrange a field trip for students to learn how produce is kept fresh for consumers.

PERISHABLE PEAS RECORD SHEET

Name(s) _____ Experiment Started _____

DIRECTIONS

1. Give one bag to your teacher to be kept in school. Take the other bag home and put it in your freezer. Record your observations of the contents of each bag on the chart below. Pay attention to changes in color and texture.

2. Use a thermometer to check the temperature in your freezer on the day you begin your experiment. Leave the thermometer in the freezer for 15 to 20 minutes and then record the temperature here: _____

3. Make a prediction about how this experiment will turn out.

_____

_____

DATE	OBSERVATIONS OF FROZEN PRODUCE	OBSERVATIONS OF UNFROZEN PRODUCE
DAY 4		
DAY 8		
DAY 12		
DAY 16		

Based on your observations, write a statement on a separate piece of paper about the effects of freezing on perishable products. Use data from your experiment to support your conclusions.

ANCIENT ARTIFACTS

OBJECTIVE

The purpose of this lesson is to research and re-create artifacts from ancient arctic cultures.

PROCEDURE

1. Define the term *artifact* and discuss with the class what we can learn about a culture from its artifacts. What can an artifact reveal about people and their environment? Also discuss the role of an archaeologist in recovering and interpreting uses of artifacts. Use a map to review cultures that live in arctic climates. Some specific groups to study might be the Aleut, Haida, Laps, Inuit, or Micmac.

2. Brainstorm a list of artifacts with the class. Some categories are tools, jewelry, and clothing. Specific examples of items for these categories include masks, umiaks, parkas, mukluks, ulus, bolas, and leisters.

3. Tell the students that they are going to become archaeologists and research an ancient arctic civilization to find and then re-create artifacts. Divide the class into groups

4. Each group of student archaeologists should create a discovery box that will be presented to the class. This box should contain reproduced artifacts. The groups will share their research findings on the origins and purpose of each of the artifacts.

5. Pass out and review the research worksheet.

6. Allow the students class time to research their artifacts, using classroom references, the library or media center, and the Internet if possible. Monitor students' research. Provide specific leads, if needed.

7. Have students present their discovery boxes. Have the class discuss what each artifact reveals about the people's way of life and their environment.

ANCIENT ARTIFACTS *(continued)*

EXTENSIONS

1. Have students brainstorm a list of important artifacts from our culture and then describe what future archaeologists could learn from each artifact. This activity could be done as a warm-up to the lesson described above.

2. Create an archeological dig, using a large plastic garbage can full of sand or Styrofoam packing nuggets. Each student should bring in one artifact from their grandparents' culture. Students should analyze one another's artifacts.

3. Have students create a time capsule, which will be buried on school property. Each student should bring in an artifact that reveals something about modern American culture. Have students come up with a method for packing the materials to preserve them over time and create a map for a future class to unearth the capsule.

4. Ask students to research famous archaeologists and discuss the effect of their major discoveries on society.

5. Compare artifacts from one culture to another. Discuss the role of natural resources in the construction of artifacts.

ANCIENT ARTIFACTS

Archaeologists _____

DIRECTIONS

Use this sheet as a guide to complete your discovery box. Organize your research using the following chart. When you are finished with research, you will be re-creating these artifacts to put in your discovery box.

ARTIFACT	MATERIALS	USE

Make a list of materials you will need to re-create three artifacts. Decide how the materials will be obtained and the artifacts constructed. Divide these responsibilities among team members.

Artifact 1 _____

_____

Artifact 2 _____

_____

Artifact 3 _____

_____

MAKING TRACKS

The purpose of this lesson is for students to research particular arctic animal traits and to use the information to design a set of arctic animal tracks.

1. Provide students with encyclopedias, wildlife cards, or other sources to locate information about animals.

2. Ask students to close their eyes and take an imaginary trip into the past: "Imagine you are an Inuit hunter living in the Arctic 200 years ago. People in your village are hungry. You have been hunting for three days with no success. You are tired and hungry yourself. Suddenly you come upon a set of animal tracks. Do you follow them?"

3. Elicit responses from students. Ask them what criteria they think the hunter would set before making a decision about the tracks. (Will this animal provide food? How many animals are there? How old are the tracks?) Discuss how survival depended upon the ability to track animals for food.

4. Pass out copies of the Making Tracks worksheet. Monitor research and provide leads if necessary.

5. When students have completed the activity, discuss ways that scientists use tracking today. (Migration patterns, animal behavior, determining population status of endangered species, and so on.)

From *Living with the Land*, Copyright © 1998 Good Year Books.

MAKING TRACKS *(continued)*

EXTENSIONS

1. Have students create an arctic food chain bulletin board by drawing animal tracks and captions with the animals' names on them.

2. Have students create an animal "track map" in a sandy area near school where local animals are known to frequent. For example, scatter some seeds in a smooth patch of sand and return periodically to see if there are any bird tracks in the sand. Draw pictures of the tracks and use resources to identify the animal that might have made the prints.

3. Have students create replicas of arctic animal tracks in plaster of Paris and write informative captions about the animals on index cards. Display work in the library or hallway showcase.

4. Give each student six 4-by-3-inch pieces of paper and a paper bag. Using the information from their research notes, have them write single-word clues about the animal on each piece of paper. Encourage them to select descriptive words about the animal. Have students exchange bags. Pulling the clues out one at a time, they should try to guess the animal's name, using the fewest clues.

5. Ask students to use the information from the research sheet to write acrostic poems about the arctic animals.

From *Living with the Land*, Copyright © 1998 Good Year Books.

MAKING TRACKS

Name(s) _____

Long ago, survival in arctic regions depended on tracking and hunting skills. Choose an animal from the list below. Research the traits listed, and use the information to help you design a set of animal tracks in the box at the bottom of the page.

ARCTIC ANIMALS

caribou	arctic fox	arctic hare	stoat
lemming	polar bear	snowy owl	puffin

Animal: _____

TRAITS

1. How is the animal's foot shaped? Is it like a hoof, a paw, a claw, and so on?

   _____

2. How does the animal move? Does it leap, walk, hop, and so on?

   _____

3. What is the average weight and height of the animal? Use this information to help you determine the size of prints and the distance between tracks.

   _____

4. List other helpful information._____

When you are done, cut out the box at the right. Exchange prints with another student. See if you can use the information about tracking to figure out what animal made the set of prints.

ALL DRESSED UP

OBJECTIVE

The purpose of this lesson is for students to learn about the use of natural resources in the arctic climate. They will research information, record it in note form, and use data to develop a product to present to the class.

PROCEDURE

1. Collect supplemental research materials from the library or media center or sign up the class to do research in the library or media center. Tap into on-line resources if possible.

2. Review information about the climate in arctic regions, emphasizing winter temperatures. How did people keep warm and survive in such a harsh climate hundreds of years ago?

3. Pass out the All Dressed Up worksheet. Ask students where they would look to locate information to complete the sheet. Make a list of suggestions on the chalkboard or on the overhead projector. This activity may be done individually, in pairs, or in small groups at the teacher's discretion.

4. Monitor the research, guiding student choice of supplemental materials.

5. When research is completed, discuss products that students can make and present to the class. Brainstorm with class a materials-needed list. Encourage students to bring in extra materials to share with classmates.

6. Provide class time for construction of products, peer-presentation practice, and presentation of final products.

EXTENSIONS

1. Have students record audiotapes describing the products they created. Students can create a self-guided tour of products displayed around the room. Invite other classes to take the "tour."

2. Use the worksheet as a model to branch off into other topics. For example, students might research Inuit tools such as the harpoon, ulu, and fishing net.

3. Have students design futuristic arctic clothing.

4. Ask students to write and illustrate a "how-to" book for creating an article of Inuit clothing.

5. Have students prepare a packing list of clothing needed for a month-long trip to the North Pole by dogsled.

ALL DRESSED UP

Name(s) _____

DIRECTIONS

Research each article of clothing below. Record your notes in the correct box.

ARTICLE OF CLOTHING	WHAT MATERIAL WAS IT MADE FROM?	HOW WAS IT USED?
Parka		
Mukluks		
Snowshoes		

How would you like to present the information you learned to the class?

____ Make Inuit clothes and dress a doll with them.

____ Make a poster, with captions illustrating the clothing.

____ Make a picture book showing how the clothing was used.

____ Other. Write a project description below:

_____

_____

_____

_____

ARCTIC CIRCLE

OBJECTIVE

The purpose of this lesson is for students to use mapping skills, particularly the use of scale, direction, and reference points, to plan a flight over the Arctic Circle.

PROCEDURE

1. Obtain a map of the Arctic Circle for each pair of students. Some atlases contain this map. Set up students to work in pairs.

2. Ask the students if they have ever taken a trip in an airplane. What tools does a pilot have available today to help reach the destination? Explain that pilots used different methods before the advent of modern technology. They used a combination of *pilotage* and *dead reckoning*. *Pilotage* refers to the use of visual reference points, or checkpoints, that a pilot would expect to see along the route. *Dead reckoning* refers to the direction of flight and the speed of the aircraft between known positions (checkpoints). Tell students that today they will be pilots planning a flight through the Arctic Circle.

3. Review the use of scale and the compass rose. Using the wall map, model directions given on the worksheet using this example, with the departure point of Havana, Cuba, and the destination of Manaus, Brazil.

CHECKPOINT

Havana, Cuba	Direction	Distance
Jamaica	SE	500 miles
Caracas	SE	850 miles
Angel Falls	SE	475 miles
Fork of Branco & Negro Rivers	S	500 miles
Manaus, Brazil	SE	200 miles

4. Remind students to estimate distance. Discuss other possible routes and checkpoints.

5. Hand out a copy of the Arctic Circle worksheet to each pair of students.

From *Living with the Land*, Copyright © 1998 Good Year Books.

6. When students have completed their flight plans, check work for accuracy. Discuss the importance of using accurate directions and distance measurements in transportation-related careers.

EXTENSIONS

1. Make copies of an Arctic Circle map for each pair of students. Have them exchange flight plans and highlight the route on the map.

2. Contact a local airport and try to find a pilot who is willing to demonstrate the use of a real flight plan to the class.

3. Have the students create a map for a different mode of transportation through the Arctic Circle, such as by dogsled, truck, snowmobile, or on foot.

4. Ask students to create a log with entries about what they did and saw along the route.

5. Have students create a riddle game using different locations in the Arctic Circle. Using an atlas, the students should write degrees of latitude and longitude for particular places on index cards (with answers on the back). Classmates should try to find the name of the location using a wall map.

ARCTIC CIRCLE

Copilots _____

Use a map of the Arctic Circle to plan your flight. Your point of departure and destination must be in or near the Arctic Circle. Use as checkpoints visual reference points such as bodies of water, land features, roads, or cities to help you reach your destination safely. Remember to list your checkpoints in order, or you might wind up in the middle of the Arctic Ocean with no fuel!

FLIGHT PLAN

Point of departure _____

Destination _____

CHECKPOINT

	Direction	Distance

File this flight plan with your chief pilot (teacher)
to see if you reached your destination successfully!
Good luck!

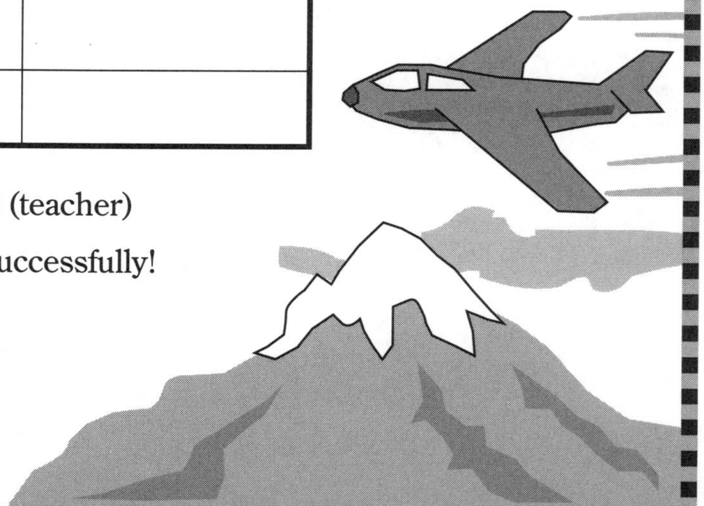

POLAR GLOW

OBJECTIVE

The purpose of this lesson is for students to investigate and compare the aurora borealis to another natural phenomenon.

PROCEDURE

1. Obtain multiple copies of a scientific description of the aurora borealis. Collect library or media materials relating to other natural phenomena for class research.

2. Read the following verse to the class:

> *Far north where there's always snow,*
> *You will see the polar glow.*
> *Streaks of color flashing high,*
> *Lighting up the arctic sky.*

   What is the author describing? Brainstorm ideas with the class and list them on the chalkboard or an overhead.

3. Define and discuss the term natural phenomenon with the class. Explain to students that they will research a natural phenomenon called the aurora borealis that occurs in arctic regions.

4. Ask students to think of other natural phenomena they have experienced or learned about. Make a list, using the overhead projector or the chalkboard. The list should include such examples as tornado, lightning, hurricane, sirocco, flood, and earthquake. Ask students where they would look to find information on these phenomena.

5. Set up pairs or small groups for research. Pass out copies of the description of the aurora borealis and the "Polar Glow" worksheet to each group. Review the use of Venn diagrams to compare similarities and differences.

6. When students are finished, have them compare data with other groups, making needed revisions or additions.

EXTENSIONS

1. Review the use of rhyme and meter in poetry. Have groups use data from the chart to create four- or eight-line poems to describe their favorite phenomenon.

2. Have students create a legend to explain the origins of a natural phenomenon.

3. Ask students to collect old magazines, particularly nature magazines, to create a giant collage of different types of natural phenomena entitled "The Forces of Nature."

4. Have students research a specific event, such as the eruption of Mount St. Helens, and write a newspaper article.

5. Have students choose a phenomenon with disastrous side effects and write a disaster survival guide.

POLAR GLOW

Researchers _____

The aurora borealis is nature's light show in the Arctic. Choose another natural phenomenon you want to know more about and write it in the circle. Research both, and complete the diagram below.

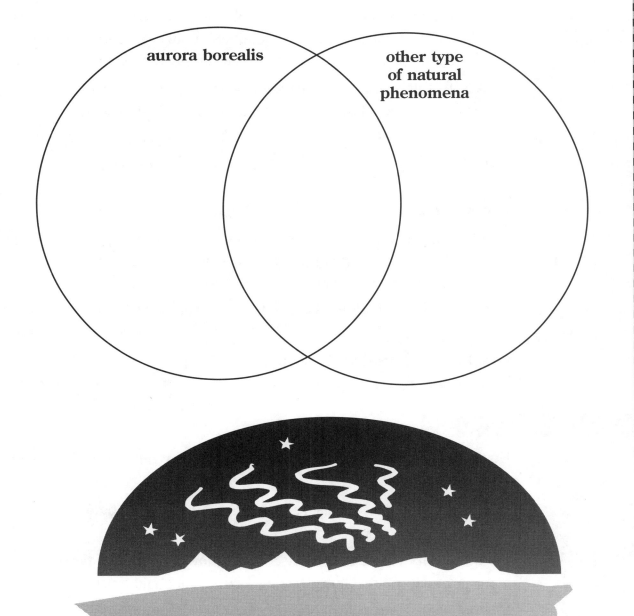

aurora borealis

other type
of natural
phenomena

WHALE WATCHERS

OBJECTIVE

The purpose of this lesson is to have students track whale migration using latitude and longitude.

PROCEDURE

1. Ask students if they know of any animal that travels south during the winter months. Elicit responses that include different animals. Discuss why the students think these animals leave their homes during different parts of the year.

2. Explain that what these animals are doing is called *migration*. Discuss what migration means and how animals migrate—that is, that they fly, run, or swim.

3. Tell students that they will pretend to be scientists tracking whales. They are going to track where whales have been sighted using degrees of latitude and longitude.

4. Review latitude and longitude on a wall map.

5. Hand out the Whale Watchers worksheet and a piece of acetate. Explain to students that they are going to lay the acetate over the map in the atlas and mark the points where whales have been sighted.

6. Allow students to work independently or in groups. Monitor their progress.

7. Have students share predictions of where they think the next whale sighting will be. How did they reach their conclusions?

> **NOTE:** Students must know how to locate latitude and longitude to complete this worksheet. Their prediction should be based on the other locations listed on the worksheet.

EXTENSIONS

1. Have students write journal entries on what they did and saw on a whale watch in the Arctic.

2. Have students create a treasure map using degrees of latitude and longitude as clues.

3. Have students create and label a chart showing different types of whale behavior, such as breaching, making a bubble net, and fluke slapping.

4. Have students create a migration story from the animal's point of view. Encourage them to use all of the senses to describe the animal's adventures.

From *Living with the Land*, Copyright © 1998 Good Year Books.

WHALE WATCHERS

Sighting Crew: _____

You have been chosen to join a team of biologists to research whale sightings. You will plot the following four spottings using degrees of latitude and longitude. Your research ship, *Fluke Splash*, has left Newfoundland and is proceeding in a southerly direction.

LATITUDE	LONGITUDE
1. 46°N	55°W
2. 43°N	61°W
3. 35°N	70°W
4. 30°N	75°W

Stop! Your gas is getting low. You must now predict when and where the whales will be sighted next.

_____

_____

_____

_____

_____

_____

From *Living with the Land*, Copyright © 1998 Good Year Books.

ARCTIC GLOSSARY

Name(s) _____

Arctic: A term that describes frigid polar regions.

Arctic Circle: A line of latitude 66-1/2 degrees North that marks the northern polar region.

Artifact: An object, such as a tool, from an ancient culture.

Baleen: Sheets of fingernail-like material inside some whales' mouths; used for catching food such as krill or squid.

Bering Strait: The narrow body of water that separates Alaska from Asia.

Blubber: Thick layer of fat that protects whale in arctic water.

Bola: A tool made of leather strips and rocks used to catch ducks.

Eskimos: The name given to the natives who settled in the arctic region of North America.

Iditarod: An annual dogsled race that begins in Alaska and honors the people and dogs who saved Nome, a town in Alaska, from diphtheria in 1925.

Igloo: A temporary winter shelter made of ice; Inuit built them on hunting trips.

Inuit: The name the Eskimos call themselves. It means "the people."

Leister: A spear used for fishing.

Mukluks: Boots made of waterproof animal skin.

Muktuk: The blubber of a whale; used for food by Inuit.

Parka: A fur jacket worn by Inuit; usually made of seal- or caribou skin.

Permafrost: Arctic soil that is always frozen and never thaws.

Reference point: The point from which we measure direction or distance. For example, in the question "Is Georgia north of Florida?" Florida is the reference point.

Shaman: A person who served as a combination doctor and priest for a tribe.

Strait: A narrow body of water that joins two larger bodies of water.

Tundra: Flat, treeless, arctic area with permafrost, where only lichens, moss, and shrubs grow.

Ulu: A curved knife with a palm-held handle used for separating blubber from skin on sea mammals.

Umiak: An open boat Inuit use to hunt whales.

PLAINS
REGIONS

Plains are regions of rolling lands in temperate climates. Grasses outnumber all other plants. Plains are called grasslands or prairies in North America, steppes in Eurasia, and the pampas in Argentina.

The climate in plains regions varies from winter temperatures below freezing to summer temperatures as high as 100 degrees Fahrenheit. Differing amounts of precipitation cause conditions ranging from droughts to floods. Strong winds and storms are common in these regions.

Grasses have traits that help them thrive and maintain natural boundaries. One-half or more of each plant grows beneath the soil. Fires started by lightning and spread by strong winds can kill trees and shrubs, but fire enriches the soil and seems to stimulate the growth of grass.

Animals, particularly burrowing and grazing types, have adapted to plains regions. The prairie dog is common in North America. Native American groups such as the Cheyenne and Sioux depended upon the American bison, or buffalo, for survival. The introduction of the horse by Spanish settlers enabled Native Americans to extend their hunting range. The buffalo was brought to the brink of extinction as European settlers moved west across the Great Plains.

Plains regions are the most important food producing areas of the world. Most grain crops, such as corn or wheat, are grown in these regions. Cattle and sheep graze on grasslands. Overgrazing and the use of chemicals for crop cultivation are issues concerning environmentalists today.

PLAINS REGIONS

THE DISAPPEARING BUFFALO

OBJECTIVES

The purpose of this lesson is to review the destructive effect of the decline of the buffalo on the lives of Native American tribes living on the Great Plains. Students will interpret information and use it to create graphs.

PROCEDURE

1. Ask students to brainstorm the many, varied, and unusual ways Plains Indians used the buffalo. Discuss the importance of the buffalo to their daily existence.

2. Tell the students they are going to read a story about the decline of the buffalo during the 1800s in the Great Plains region. Explain that they will use the information they read to create a line graph representing the change in the number of buffalo over time.

3. Explain that a line graph shows change over a period of time. It must have a horizontal axis and vertical axis that are labeled. It must also have a title.

4. Read the story "The Disappearing Buffalo" (on the following page) to students, or have them read it independently.

5. Ask students to locate and highlight important dates and numbers in the story.

6. Pass out graph paper to students. Students should work independently or with a partner to create a line graph using the information found in the story.

7. Have students share the graphs with the class. Discuss the different titles and labeling formats chosen.

EXTENSIONS

1. Have students create line graph representing the number of buffalo on the Great Plains in the last ten years.

2. Have students create a different type of graph, such as a pie graph, a pictograph, or a bar graph.

3. Have students create a legend to explain why a white buffalo is considered sacred by many Native American tribes.

4. Have students create an advertising poster for a railroad company in 1850.

5. Ask students to pretend they are a members of a Sioux or Cheyenne tribe and to write a song or poem about the loss of the buffalo.

THE DISAPPEARING BUFFALO

Name(s) _____

The whistle blew loudly in the early morning hours on a spring day in 1870. The settlers living on the Great Plains were excited to be boarding this new and unique mode of transportation. It could hold many people and travel across the entire United States in days. This great invention was called the railroad. It spanned the country from New York to San Francisco, slicing a path through the prairie.

The tracks stretched across vast grasslands where the once-bountiful buffalo grazed. Years ago, enormous herds roamed as far as the eye could see. They provided food, shelter, tools, and clothing for Plains tribes. Now the buffalo was on the verge of extinction. How could such a change happen in such a short amount of time?

In 1830, there were 75 million buffalo living on the Great Plains. While the railroad was being constructed, the number of buffalo began to diminish. The buffalo was food for the large camps of men laying down iron rails. Buffalo hunters took the hides that brought them money, while leaving the carcasses to rot.

By 1850, there were 50 million buffalo roaming the prairie and causing major traffic problems for the railroads. Ten-mile-long herds were crossing the tracks, delaying trains for hours or even days. The railroads hired professional shooters to begin the slaughter of the buffalo. Farmers and cattle drivers joined the railroads in killing off the buffalo.

By 1880, the total number of buffalo living on the Great Plains had dropped to fewer than 1,000. The animal that many tribes depended upon had all but disappeared. How could the Plains tribes survive?

From *Living with the Land*, Copyright © 1998 Good Year Books.

LEGENDS OF LONG AGO

OBJECTIVE

The purpose of this lesson is for students to identify key elements of a legend and to create original Native American legends.

PROCEDURE

1. Invite students to summarize any legends they know for the class. How are legends different from other stories?

2. Explain that all legends contain certain elements. Legends

    - Explain natural events in a fictional rather than scientific way.

    - Take place long ago.

    - Are in story form, having been passed down from one generation to the next by word of mouth.

3. Many Native American legends have been rewritten in recent years. Read one or two aloud to the class, and have them identify the elements of legends. Two possible choices are *Dancing Drum* by Terri Cohlene and the *Legend of the Blue Bonnet* by Tomie dePaola.

4. Have students read "The Boastful Sun" and complete the worksheet independently. They should save the worksheet to use later as a warm-up for a group activity.

5. Brainstorm with the class a list of natural events that could be explained by legends. Some possible categories are weather, geologic formations, and bodies of water.

6. Divide the class into groups. Students should first share their responses to "The Boastful Sun." Groups should then choose a natural event to explain in their legend. Direct students to brainstorm a number of possible explanations before they begin to write the legends. Have students share the final versions with the class.

7. To increase student accountability, you may choose to use the Legend Checklist.

From *Living with the Land*, Copyright © 1998 Good Year Books.

LEGENDS OF LONG AGO *(continued)*

EXTENSIONS

1. Have students write a letter to a major motion picture company like Disney or Universal Studios explaining why their legend should be made into a movie. Remind them to send a copy of the legend.

2. Bring in natural objects such as fruit or leaves, and have each student write a legend.

3. Have students read more Native American legends and mark the tribe's location on a map of North America.

4. Have students dress in Native American costumes and tell legends to a younger class.

THE BOASTFUL SUN ECLIPSED

by Mary S. Gates

Name(s) _____

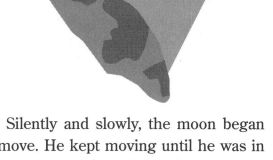

Long ago, when the universe was new and time had just begun, the sun was young and proud. As his light reached out through the solar system, he became more impressed with his ability to light up the planets beyond.

One day the young sun began bragging to his neighbor, the moon. "Look at how my light illuminates everything in my sight. If it were not for me, everything would be plunged into darkness. No one would ever see you, Old Moon."

The wise moon knew there were more powerful suns in the universe, but he did not wish to upset his friend, so he said, "Your light is very powerful indeed."

As time went on, the sun became more intrigued with his own talents. Solar flares erupted when he flexed his muscles. He thought distant stars were puny because their light was so dim.

He turned to the moon one day and proudly stated, "I am the giver of all light. I am most powerful. Nothing would exist without me. Every creature in the universe should honor me."

The moon realized the arrogant sun was heading for trouble. He decided to do something before the sun became impossible to live with. Like a wise scholar, he pondered the problem for awhile. He smiled to himself when he thought of a brilliant plan to bring the sun back to his senses.

Silently and slowly, the moon began to move. He kept moving until he was in front of the sun, blocking his magnificent light to the Earth.

"What have you done?" howled the sun. "You've blocked my sparkling radiance! I'm as powerless as a rock!"

"Your light is powerful, my friend, but don't waste time basking in your own glory. Use your power to help others," said the moon.

At first the sun was bewildered. He considered the words of his enlightened friend, and it dawned on him that he'd been quite selfish.

"I have been rather boastful," murmured the sun. "From now on, I shall use my energy to help others."

The moon slid away allowing the rays of the sun to show the beautiful colors of the watery planet beyond. "Just to remind you of your promise," said the moon solemnly, "I will move to block your light from time to time. You will remember that without the worlds around you, your light would be meaningless."

And to this day you can still see an eclipse . . . from time to time!

LEGEND CHECKLIST

Name _____ Due Date _____

Use this checklist to make sure all elements are done before you hand your piece in to be graded. Attach this grade sheet to your work.

Student Check	Points Lost	Elements Required
		Explains something in nature in a fictional, not scientific way. [20 points]
		It happened long ago. [10 points]
		It is a fictional story with characters, action, and a setting. [30 points]
		The story is told in the third person, like a story being passed down from one generation to the next. [10 points]
		Include two similes. [10 points] [A simile is a comparison using the words *like* or *as*.]
		Show there is a clear problem and solution. [20 points]

*** You Will Lose **2 Points** for Every Mechanics Error. ***

Content Grade: [ ]   Mechanics Grade: [ ]

Teacher Comments:

SCALED DOWN TO SIZE

OBJECTIVE

The purpose of this lesson is to give students practice measuring map scale in kilometers and miles, using cities found in the Plains states.

PROCEDURE

1. Provide rulers and maps of the United States or atlases for each group. Students may work in pairs or small groups, depending on the materials you have available.

2. Using a wall map, review the concept of scale. Review estimation skills in math. Emphasize that scale gives an approximate rather than an exact measure of distance. Discuss the concept of *range,* explaining that while some answers may differ, they should be within a particular range.

3. Pass out materials and copies of the Scaled Down to Size worksheet. As you circulate among groups, monitor measuring techniques. Have groups compare answers when finished.

EXTENSIONS

1. Get a number of travel brochures from a local travel agent. Ask students to plan a "dream" trip and calculate the round-trip mileage.

2. Have students contact a school in a different climate on the Internet. Each class should create travel brochures for its town and send them via e-mail to each other.

3. Have the students calculate how long it would take to reach a specific destination using various modes of transportation.

4. Have students write and illustrate short biographies of famous people who have lived in Plains states.

From *Living with the Land,* Copyright © 1998 Good Year Books.

SCALED DOWN TO SIZE

Name(s) _____

You will need a map of the United States
to complete this sheet.

1. Find the scales of measurement on this map. How are the scales the same?

   _____

   How are the scales different?

   _____

2. On the map, about how many kilometers are represented by 5 centimeters?

   _____

   About how many miles are represented by 6 inches? _____

3. A new student has joined the class and has never studied scale on maps. How
   would you explain it to him or her?

   _____

   _____

   _____

4. How would the new student measure the distance from Pierre, South Dakota, to
   Lincoln, Nebraska?

   _____

   _____

   _____

5. A scale of measurement gives you an estimated distance between places.
   If you wanted to know the exact distance between Kirksville, Missouri, and
   Fort Dodge, Iowa, where would you look?

   _____

   _____

   _____

Name(s) _____

6. Using the metric scale, what is the estimated length of North Dakota?

    _____

    What is the estimated width of South Dakota? _____

    What is the estimated length of the Missouri River? (Hint: The source is in
    northern Montana.) _____

    What is the estimated length of Oklahoma's northern border?

    _____

7. Using the scale of miles, what is the estimated length of Lake Michigan?

    _____

    What is the estimated perimeter of Kansas? _____

    What is the estimated distance from Kansas City, Missouri, to Portland, Oregon?

    _____

    What is the estimated distance from Odessa, Texas, to Minot, North Dakota?

    _____

8. Two natural boundaries of the Great Plains are the Rocky Mountains and the
    Mississippi River. About how many kilometers apart are these two natural
    formations? _____

9. Find three tribal reservations on the Great Plains using your map or any other
    source. Measure the distance between them. About how many miles would you
    drive in order to visit all three reservations? _____

10. How does the Great Plains compare in size to the Sahara Desert?

    _____

    _____

    _____

From *Living with the Land*, Copyright © 1998 Good Year Books.

JOURNAL JOURNEYS

OBJECTIVE

The purpose of this lesson is for students to recognize the importance of the westward expansion to different groups, using research and note-taking skills.

PROCEDURE

1. Explain that many different people lived on and relied on the Great Plains region, or prairie, from 1830 to 1890. Some groups to discuss are Plains warriors, settlers, miners, ranchers, railroad workers, and the U.S. Cavalry.

2. Tell students that they are going to research one of these groups to find reasons why the Great Plains region was important to them.

3. Explain that each group had its own point of view about the region and its resources. It will be their job to find information that explain a particular group's point of view.

4. Set up groups. Students research and record data. The information they find will be the basis for three journal entries to be done by each group.

5. Read a few journal entries from the book *An Indian Winter* by Russell Freedman to help the students understand the format of a journal entry.

6. Review each group's notes for accuracy and detail before they begin to write journal entries.

7. Students write journal entries and share them with the class.

EXTENSIONS

1. Have the students create a skit to go along with their journal entries.

2. Have students read about Buffalo Bill Cody's Wild West show and create posters advertising the show.

3. Ask students to draw a diagram of a typical army post in the 1800s.

JOURNAL JOURNEYS

Group members: _____

DIRECTIONS

Use available resources to find out about the life style of the character you have
been assigned. Use your notes to write three journal entries from the character's
point of view. Be sure to include year and location.

I am a _____ .

The prairie is important to me because

_____

_____

_____

My journal entries are

_____
_____
_____

_____
_____
_____

_____
_____
_____

CHANGING TIMES

OBJECTIVE

The purpose of this lesson is for students to investigate events from 1830 to 1890 from two points of view: that of Plains tribes and that of white settlers. Students will analyze these points of view through the creation of a comparative time-line.

PROCEDURE

1. Gather resource materials that cover American history during the nineteenth century. Be sure to include materials about Native American tribes living in the Plains region.

2. Read the story "Changing Times" to the class. Who behaved savagely; the Plains tribes or the soldiers? Discuss the concept of point of view, emphasizing how it can influence our perceptions.

3. Review the concept of a time line using yourself or a student as a model. Note how important dates and events are emphasized.

4. Organize students in groups. Give each group copies of both the "Changing Times" story and worksheet. Direct groups to make a plan for locating information before they start their research.

5. When students complete the time lines, provide time for them to share their research with the class. Post time lines around the room.

EXTENSIONS

1. Have students use the information in the time lines to write two stories, one from the point of view of the settlers and one from the point of view of the Plains tribes.

2. Ask students to write and perform a skit about a famous chief or battle.

3. Divide the class into teams to debate who was more "savage": the Plains tribes or the cavalry soldiers. Then reverse sides to debate again.

4. Have students make a time-line poster of famous Plains tribal leaders and include pictures and events from their lives. Some possible leaders are Crazy Horse, Spotted Tail, Plenty Coup, Crowfoot, Washakie, and Sitting Bull.

5. Have students research and construct a map of a famous engagement, such as Sand Creek, Little Big Horn, or Wounded Knee.

CHANGING TIMES

Group Investigators _____

DIRECTIONS

Use the information from the "Changing Times" story as a starting place for your research. Use varied sources to learn about people and events relating to the settlement of the West between 1830 and 1890.

Record your notes below. Use your research to construct two time lines; one from the Plains tribes' point of view and one from the settlers' point of view.

PLAINS TRIBES   **SETTLERS**

_____

_____

_____

_____

_____

_____

CHANGING TIMES

Name(s) _____

During the later part of the nineteenth century, many American citizens called on the government to protect settlers moving West. Stories of innocent white settlers being murdered and scalped by Indians gave people nightmares. Some people declared, "The only good Indian is a dead Indian." They wanted the "savages" eradicated.

Who were these "savage" tribes? Why did they treat white settlers so badly? It is impossible to summarize this period of history in a few paragraphs, but here is the story of one tribal leader.

Black Kettle was a brave Cheyenne warrior, scout, and tribal leader who fought against enemy tribes, such as the Ute and Pawnee. The white settlers had more warriors and more powerful weapons than any tribe he had fought. Like many other tribal leaders, he felt that the only way to save his people was to make peace with the white man. In 1851, he signed a peace treaty with the U.S. government. He hoped that his people and the white settlers could coexist in peace. Black Kettle and his people were forced to live on a reservation in Sand Creek, Colorado, on land too poor to farm and with too little game to hunt.

White settlers continued to hunt on Cheyenne land. Interaction between settlers and natives exposed the tribe to illnesses, such as smallpox and influenza, that killed many of their people. In retaliation, the tribe conducted raids on the settlers.

Black Kettle went to Washington, D.C., to plead for a better life for his people. However, the Civil War had started, and there were few resources for native tribes. The Cheyenne continued to raid the farms of the white settlers and attacked stage coaches.

In 1864, Major Scott Anthony and Colonel John Chivington attacked Black Kettle's camp at Sand Creek, Colorado, killing four hundred to five hundred men, women, and children. Black Kettle signed another treaty with the government, and his people were forced to move to a new reservation. White settlers and enemy tribes continued to attack, so he took his people to stay with the Kiowa tribe.

In 1868, Black Kettle traveled to Fort Cobb in Oklahoma with other Cheyenne and Arapaho leaders in an attempt to improve living conditions for his people. The Seventh Cavalry, led by Colonel George Armstrong Custer, discovered Black Kettle's camp at Washita River, Oklahoma. Black Kettle and his wife rode out to meet the soldiers. Black Kettle carried an American flag in his hand as a gesture of peace, but he and his wife were shot and killed. The soldiers attacked the camp, killing about one hundred people, only eleven of whom were warriors.

THE SHRINKING LAND

OBJECTIVE

The purpose of this lesson is for students to use acquired knowledge and a set of criteria to design a future mode of mass transportation.

PROCEDURE

1. Using a wall map of the United States, outline the Oregon Trail from Independence, Missouri, to Portland, Oregon. Discuss how mass transportation has changed since the days of the Conestoga wagon. How have changes in technology affected the way people live?

2. Discuss the term *criteria* with the class. Ask them to imagine that your school is hiring a new principal. What criteria would they like to see used in the hiring process? List their ideas on chart paper.

3. Set up groups, pass out copies of the The Shrinking Land worksheet and review directions with the class.

4. Monitor group interaction, making sure they focus on the task and refer often to the set of criteria.

5. When groups are finished, have them present their ideas to the class. Tell the class that they are executives of the transportation company. Ask them to judge the merits of each concept presented, using only the set of criteria outlined in the lesson.

EXTENSIONS

1. Have the class choose the most promising group design and build a model.

2. Ask students to construct a set of criteria for high school graduation. Compare the results with your district policy.

3. Show the class a television program that focuses on new trends in technology. Have the class design items that could be featured on the show twenty years from now.

4. Have students interview a relative to find out what criteria were used by their employer when they were hired for their present position.

5. Ask students to come up with a new word and write a definition for a dictionary fifty years in the future.

From *Living with the Land*, Copyright © 1998 Good Year Books.

THE SHRINKING LAND

Engineering Team Members _____

In the early 1800s, the land between Independence, Missouri, and Portland, Oregon, was a wild frontier. Settlers moving west on the Oregon Trail endured months of hardship to reach their destination. By 1870, the transcontinental railroad system was running and the trip from Independence to Portland took days instead of months. After World War II, travel by plane became more common. Commercial jets today can cover that same distance in just a few hours.

You have been hired by a major transportation company to design a futuristic mode of transportation. They have established a set of criteria, or guidelines, you must follow:

• The mode of transportation must be inexpensive to construct and operate.

• The mode of transportation must have a minimal impact on the environment.

• The mode of transportation must be economical and easily accessible to consumers.

Brainstorm ideas for each category below.

Possible materials	Possible sources of energy

Keeping the set of criteria in mind, design your futuristic mode of transportation on a separate piece of paper. Use labels and captions to explain your work.

TO YOUR HEALTH

OBJECTIVES

The purpose of this lesson is to introduce students to the role of shaman, or medicine man, and for students to research plants that were used by tribes for healing.

PROCEDURE

1. Gather resources on American plants and herbs from the library or media center, or sign up for time for students to do research. If possible, use the Internet to access additional information.

2. Read the following paragraph to the class to introduce the topic:

> *Healing rituals were common among Plains tribes. They were performed by a shaman, or medicine man, who was a valuable member of the tribal community. The shaman used herbs, spells, potions, and ointments like an artist uses paints. Sometimes a shaman would enter a trance to help his patient. His "spirit" left his body and sought out the "spirit" or soul of his patient. If he successfully contacted the spirit, he tried to heal it and rid the body of illness or demons.*

3. Brainstorm with the class a list of herbs or plants they think Plains tribes may have used for healing purposes. List ideas on the board or use an overhead projector.

4. Set up research groups. Pass out copies of the To Your Health worksheet to each group. Provide research leads if necessary. Monitor research for accuracy of information.

5. When the worksheet is completed, have students share their descriptions of illnesses and treatment plans with classmates.

EXTENSIONS

1. Have students plant a vegetable or herb garden. Students should harvest their crop when the plants mature and use the ingredients to make a meal.

2. Ask the class to make a plant book with pen-and-ink drawings and descriptions of local plants.

3. Have students research plants that are currently used to cure modern illnesses. An example is periwinkle from the rain forest, which is used to treat cancer.

4. Invite a local pharmacist to discuss the history of pharmacological medicine.

5. Have students research the history of the U.S. Food and Drug Administration and make a time line to record major events.

TO YOUR HEALTH

Researchers_____

DIRECTIONS

Choose five plants from
the list below to research.
Record your findings in
the petals of the flower.

PLANTS

Sassafras

Goldenseal

Spearmint

Joe-pye weed

Cascara sagrada

Goldenrod

Witch hazel

Datura
(jimson weed)

Pleurisy root
(butterfly weed)

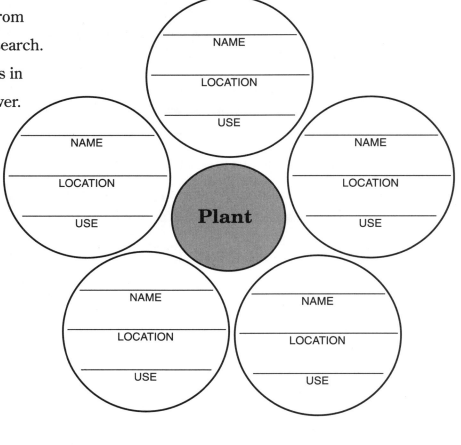

Pretend you are a shaman. In the space below, describe an illness of a member of
your tribe, and explain how you would treat it using one or more of the plants you
researched.

SYMPTOMS OF ILLNESS   **TREATMENT PLAN**

_____

_____

_____

From *Living with the Land*, Copyright © 1998 Good Year Books.

BOUNTIFUL BISON

OBJECTIVES

The purpose of this lesson is to emphasize preresearch and research skills while learning about the importance of the buffalo.

PROCEDURE

1. Gather research materials. Ask the students to think about a time when they had to do research for school. Discuss with them problems they ran into while doing research.

2. Tell them that today they will be brainstorming ways to make research easier. They will be applying those strategies to researching information about the buffalo.

3. Brainstorm with the class different resources they could use to research the buffalo, such as an encyclopedia, periodicals, books, and the Internet.

4. Ask the students what they would look up using the resources. List on the board many different possible topics for researching the buffalo—for example, bison, plains, animals, Cheyenne, Indians. Explain that by narrowing their focus using a graphic organizer, they can shorten search time. For example, reducing the general topic of "buffalo" to subcategories of "habitat" and "behavior" will help them find the information they need more quickly.

5. Tell students that they are going to use a graphic organizer to sort the information they research.

6. Review taking notes with a graphic organizer. They are to write only key words and phrases.

7. Allow the students time to fill in the graphic organizer, either independently or in groups.

8. Monitor the students' progress.

9. After the research is completed, review and discuss the sources students used for obtaining information.

BOUNTIFUL BISON *(continued)*

1. Have students create a drawing of a Plains Indian village. The village should include objects the tribe made or used from a buffalo.

2. Have students write a poem from the Cheyenne point of view honoring the buffalo.

3. Have students build a model of a travois, which was sometimes used to carry meat from a hunt back to the village.

4. Have each student paint a picture story of a buffalo hunt on the inside of a paper bag.

5. Have students make a list of objects in their home made of leather and compare them with the ways the tribes of the past used buffalo hides.

BOUNTIFUL BISON

Name(s) _____

Use resources available to gather details
to complete the organizer below.

Remember:

• Notes are key words and phrases.

• Do not write complete sentences.

• Use of abbreviation and number is okay.

Tribal uses of the buffalo

FOOD	SHELTER	TOOLS/UTENSILS
_____	_____	_____
_____	_____	_____
_____	_____	_____
_____	_____	_____
_____	_____	_____
_____	_____	_____
_____	_____	_____
_____	_____	_____

What is the most interesting fact you learned?

_____

ANIMAL ADVENTURES

OBJECTIVE

The purpose of this lesson is for students to use data to create word problems about animals found on the Great Plains.

PROCEDURE

1. Discuss how the Plains tribes used the buffalo for daily survival. Ask students how hunters determined the number of buffalo to kill so that everyone in the tribe could eat. Generate comments about determining weight.

2. Tell students that today they are going to use data about three different animals that lived on the Great Plains. They will be using data to create their own word problems. This can be done in pairs to accommodate all students.

3. Pass out copies of the Animal Adventures sheet. Read the directions aloud and discuss the data.

4. Monitor students' work, checking to make sure they follow directions.

5. When students are done writing their word problems, have each pair switch with another pair to solve the word problems.

EXTENSIONS

1. Have students research data about animals in their environment. They can use data to create a graph or word problems.

2. Ask students to write a descriptive poem about one of the animals.

3. Have students create math riddles using data about the animals.

4. Have students create a map of the United States and place animal footprints where each animal is found.

5. Plains tribes found varied uses for the buffalo. Brainstorm with the class creative uses for a liter soda bottle.

From *Living with the Land*, Copyright © 1998 Good Year Books.

ANIMAL ADVENTURES

Name(s) _____

DIRECTIONS

Write word problems using the data from the chart below. Solve the problems on scrap paper. Exchange your problems with another group and have them solve the problems, writing the answers in the box to the right.

ANIMAL	WEIGHT	RANGE OF TERRITORY	HEIGHT
BUFFALO	1,500 pounds	200 miles	6 feet
PRAIRIE DOG	2 pounds	160 acres	35 inches
PRAIRIE CHICKEN	2 pounds	100 acres	25 inches

1. Write a subtraction word problem.

_____

_____   **Solution**

_____

2. Write an addition word problem.

_____

_____   **Solution**

_____

3. Write a two-step word problem.

_____

_____   **Solution**

_____

4. Write a word problem in which you convert measurements.

_____

_____   **Solution**

_____

TRUE TREATY

OBJECTIVE

The purpose of this lesson is for students to understand historical perspective. They will use the elements of compromise to develop a treaty between Plains tribes and settlers.

PROCEDURE

1. This lesson should be done towards the end of the unit. Students need some historical knowledge of the westward movement and the Indian Wars of the later nineteenth century.

2. Ask students to talk about conflict that has occurred in their lives, in which their own opinions or interests clashed with someone else's opinions or interests. Were the conflicts resolved? How?

3. Discuss the concepts of *negotiation* and *compromise*. Explain that the process of negotiation requires parties with differing interests and opinions to meet face-to-face. The parties should clarify and discuss their views. Compromise, where both parties reach an acceptable agreement, is achieved through a give-and-take process on the part of negotiating parties. Explain that during formal meetings, negotiating parties must listen to all points of view as well as clearly express their own.

4. Explain that many treaties, or formal agreements were made between the U. S. government and the Plains tribes. Many of the treaties were broken by both sides. What caused these treaties to fail?

5. Explain that students will have an opportunity to "rewrite" history. They have been chosen by their tribe or the government to negotiate a peace treaty. Divide the class into groups. Each group should have at least six negotiators—three for each side.

6. Pass out copies of the True Treaty worksheet and review the requirements with each group. Depending on whether students are representing Native American tribes or settlers, give them a copy of the perspectives cards on page 116. They should use the cards to guide them in developing need statements.

From *Living with the Land*, Copyright © 1998 Good Year Books.

7. When all activities are completed, have each group share its treaty. Discuss strategies the groups developed to reach compromises. Does the class have insights to share on why so many treaties failed in the past?

EXTENSIONS

1. Use the strategies outlined in the lesson to address an issue of concern to students, such as wearing baseball caps in school.

2. Research a local tribe and see if any treaties are on file in your local library. Have the class compare them with the ones they developed.

3. Have students research the location and size of reservations in Great Plains states. How does the location and size of reservations compare to states in Plains regions?

4. Have students research the Bureau of Indian Affairs and investigate the historic influence of this agency on tribes.

5. Brainstorm with the class possible consequences if the nuclear test ban treaty were to be violated.

NATIVE AMERICAN PERSPECTIVE

Land is a gift, a sacred trust to be shared by all living creatures. No one person or group "owns" the land.

The economy is based on tribal survival and growth. The buffalo provides food, shelter, clothing, and utensils.

Nature is essential to religious ceremonies. Many spirits reveal themselves in animal form.

SETTLER'S PERSPECTIVE

Land is owned by individuals or groups. Deeds or claims tell who owns the land, and boundaries are marked to avoid disputes. Farming, ranching, and mining are the primary uses of land.

The economy centers around money and possessions. The more you have, the better off you are.

The main religion is Christianity, based on the belief in one God.

TRUE TREATY

Tribal Negotiators _____

Settler Negotiators _____

A treaty is a formal agreement among governments. In order for a treaty to be successful, it must meet the needs of both parties. You have been chosen to represent your people to develop a land-use treaty to bring lasting peace. Follow the steps below before you write the formal treaty.

1. Review with your team the information on the perspectives cards. Discuss how you use the land and what rights are important to the people you represent. When you have come to agreement among yourselves, list them below.

TRIBAL NEEDS	SETTLER NEEDS
_____	_____
_____	_____
_____	_____
_____	_____
_____	_____

2. Now meet with the other negotiators. Explain your needs clearly. Discuss possible solutions that will let both groups meet their needs. When you come up with ideas that seem fair to both sides, list them below.

COMPROMISE _____

_____

_____

_____

3. Use the compromise information to write a land-use treaty between the Plains tribes and the settlers. Make sure your language is clearly understood by both groups. Treaties require dates, location signed, and signatures of negotiators.

PLAINS GLOSSARY

Name(s) _____

Cheyenne: The name given to a nomadic Native American tribe living on the Plains.

Coup: A strike or hit on an enemy by a tribal warrior during a battle.

Great Plains: A large plain of central North America, covering sections of Canada and the United States.

Herd: Animals that move together in a group.

Heritage: Ideas and customs handed down by ancestors.

Little Big Horn: The place in Montana where Colonel George Armstrong Custer was defeated.

Parfleche: A leather bag used for storage.

Pemmican: Food made from berries, animal fat, and dried meat.

Plains: Flat, rolling grasslands.

Reservation: Land set aside by the government for Native Americans to live on.

Shaman: A person who was both priest and healer.

Sitting Bull: The Sioux leader who defeated Colonel Custer at Little Big Horn.

Tepee [tipi]: The type of home used by Plains Indians, made with poles and hides.

Travois: A carrier pulled by horse, dog, or people used to transport belongings.

Treaty: A formal agreement between two governments or groups.

Tribe: A group of people, bands, or villages sharing the same customs, religion, and language.

Tsitsitas: The name the Cheyenne gave themselves. It means "the people."

BIBLIOGRAPHY

DESERT

Albert, Richard E. *Alejandro's Gift*. San Francisco, CA: Chronicle Books, 1994.

Arnold, Caroline. *A Walk in the Desert*. New York: Silver Press, 1990.

Baker, Lucy. *Life in the Deserts*. New York: Scholastic, 1991.

Bash, Barbara. *Desert Giant*. New York: Little Brown and Company, 1990.

Baylor, Byrd. *The Desert Is Theirs*. New York: Macmillan, 1975.

Dewey, Jennifer Owens. *A Night and Day in the Desert*. New York: Little Brown and Company, 1991.

Sabin, Louis. *Wonders of the Desert*. Mahwah, NJ: Troll Associates, 1982.

Twist, Clint. *Deserts*. Mahwah, NJ: Troll Associates, 1991.

Wood, Audrey. *Quick as a Cricket*. Singapore: Child's Play, 1982.

RAIN FOREST

Andrews, Julia L. *Jungles and Rainforests*. New York: Explorer Books, 1991.

Baker, Jeannie. *Where the Forest Meets the Sea*. New York: Greenwillow Books, 1987.

Baker, Lucy. *Life In the Rainforest*. New York: Scholastic, 1990.

Chagnon, Napolean A. *Yanomamo*. New York: Holt, Rinehart and Winston, 1968.

Cherry, Lynne. *The Great Kapok Tree*. New York: Harcourt, 1990.

Dorros, Arthur. *Rainforest Secrets*. New York: Scholastic, 1990.

George, Jean Craighead. *One Day in the Tropical Rain Forest*. New York: HarperCollins, 1990.

Greenway, Shirley. *Jungle*. Newington, CT: Newington Press, 1991.

Illustrated Atlas of the World. Chicago: Rand McNally, 1988.

Norden, Carroll. *The Jungle*. Austin, TX: Steck-Vaughn Company, 1991.

ARCTIC

Berger, Gilda. *Whales*. New York: Doubleday, 1987.

Cohlene, Terri. *Ka-ha-si and the Loon*. Vero Beach, FL: The Rourke Corporation, 1990.

Educational Research Council of America. *The Eskimos of Northern Alaska*. Rockleigh, NJ: Allyn and Bacon, 1970.

Cohlene, Terri. *Quillworker*. Vero Beach, FL: The Rourke Corporation, 1990.

Houston, James. *Tikta' Liktak*. New York: Harcourt, 1965.

Joosse, Barbara. *Mama, Do You Love Me?* San Francisco, CA: Chronicle Books, 1991.

Khanduri, Kamini. *Polar Wildlife*. New York: Scholastic, 1992.

Munsch, Robert, and Michael Kusugak. *A Promise Is a Promise*. Toronto, Ontario, Canada: Annick Press, 1988.

Sheldon, Dyan. *The Whale's Song*. New York: Dial Books, 1991.

Smith, Greg J. H. *Eskimos*. Vero Beach, FL: The Rourke Corporation, 1990.

Standiford, Natalie. *The Bravest Dog Ever.* New York: Random House, 1989.

Wood, Jenny. *Icebergs*. New York: Scholastic, 1990.

PLAINS

Andrew, Ralph. *Curtis' Western Indians.* New York: Bonanza Books, 1962.

Brophy, William and Sophie Aberle. *The Indian.* Norman, OK: University of Oklahoma Press, 1966.

Cohlene, Terri. *Dancing Drum.* Vero Beach, FL: The Rourke Corporation Inc., 1990.

de Paola, Tomie. *The Legend of the Blue Bonnet.* New York: G. P. Putnam's Sons, 1983.

Fleishner, Jane. *Sitting Bull.* Mahwah, NJ: Troll Associates, 1979.

Fleishner, Jane. *Tecumseh.* Mahwah, NJ: Troll Associates, 1979.

Freedman, Russell. *Buffalo Hunt.* New York: Holiday House, 1981.

Freedman, Russell. *An Indian Winter.* New York: Scholastic, 1992.

Gobel, Paul. *Her Seven Brothers.* New York: Bradbury Press, 1988.

Greene, Jerome. *Battles, and Skirmishes of the Great Sioux War.* Norman, OK: University of Oklahoma Press, 1993.

Jassem, Kate. *Sacajawea.* Mahwah, NJ: Troll Associates, 1979.

Marcellin, Jean, and Jean-Robert Masson. *The Great Indian Chiefs.* New York: Barron's, 1994.

White, Jon. *Everyday Life of the North American Indians.* New York: Dorset Press, 1979.

WEB SITES

Web sites and URL addresses are subject to change at almost any time. Consult with your library or media specialist before you begin a unit of study. The specialist may have a Web site directory for educational use. You may wish to browse the Web using key words from the glossaries.

http://josnet.jostens.com/schools/kb/inuit.html
Information on Inuit environment, animals, shelter, transportation, and history

http://www.lib.uconn.edu/ArcticCircle/
Information on Arctic Circle region; natural resources, culture, virtual classroom and a chat room

http://www.nome.net/
Local and current news on Alaska

http://www.whaletimes.org/
Facts on whales and other sea creatures

http://www.euronet.nl/users/mbleeker/suri_eng.html
Suriname Rainforest; animals, plants, and people

http://www.geog.umn.edu/~schaller/amazon/
Ecuadorian Amazon Rain Forest; environment, animals, plants, and people

http://www.ran.org
Saving the rain forest

http://www.goodnet.com/~gboehm/saguaro.html
Saguaro cactus; facts and pictures

http://www.pbs.org/oregontrail/
Oregon Trail; facts, myths, and a teacher's guide